TvC

A Concise History of
British Television

Cover illustration: John Logie Baird with his television apparatus, and ventriloquist's dummy, Stooky Bill, which he used for early experimental transmissions.

A Concise History of

British Television

1930 ~ 2000

Tony Currie

Foreword by Peter Fiddick

KELLY PUBLICATIONS
6 Redlands Tiverton, Devon EX16 4DH
01884 259526
April 2000

The cartoon of Honor Blackman on page 63 is
included with the kind permission of the artist,
Richard Cole ©

Layout and design by Lynda Waller

An updated and enlarged version of
The *'Television'* Concise History of Television
as published in 7 parts in
The Journal of the Royal Television Society,
April 1995 – March 1996

First published in book-form by
KELLY PUBLICATIONS
6 Redlands, Tiverton, Devon EX16 4DH UK
April 2000

ISBN 1 903053 07 2

Contents

This book is dedicated to
four people:

HUNTER S. THOMPSON
for reminding us that
"the television business is a cruel and shallow money trench,
a long plastic hallway
where thieves and pimps run free
and good men die like dogs"

GUS MacDONALD
a wise man who knew when to quit
in favour of honest politics

SYLVIA PETERS
who has seen most of it
and remained serene throughout

and
MICHAEL GRADE
for surviving the pain and the frustrations
and still making it seem like fun.

Foreword

The history of British television no longer spans one man's working lifetime. Bill Ward, who was a teenage technician on the BBC's very first Alexandra Palace transmissions, twenty years on directed ITV's opening night, became a top programme controller, and so carried in his head the whole picture – the creativity, the technology, the politics – and died, still a programme-maker, in 1999.

Most people, even those working in or fascinated by television, do not have that historical span and can no longer hope to. There are many books but for most, life's too short. Yet there are risks in forgetting history; it's all too easily rewritten; and succeeding generations can waste an awful lot of effort reinventing the wheel.

Which is why it seemed appropriate for the Royal Television Society, as the industry's leading forum of discussion and debate, to provide a handy history, a quick guide for newcomers, a memory refresher for older hands. And since it, too, would need to span the programmes, the politics and the technology, when I commissioned it as a series of articles for the RTS's magazine, Television, *I could think of few so well equipped to write it as Tony Currie, who has an enduring interest in broadcasting, devours its output, has been a broadcaster, manager, archivist and a regulator and can drive a mixing desk. The result told me things I did not know, or had forgotten, and I am delighted that now, updated, it comes in this handy stand-alone form.*

Peter Fiddick

Editor, Television

John Logie Baird
viewing an image on one of his early televisions

Baird **with his apparatus in the Science Museum, London**

I

The Shaping of Screens to Come
The 30s

The race for innovation:
from the first fuzzy transmissions to the outbreak of war

In the beginning, television was hardly a promising entertainment prospect. From 30 September 1929 the few thousand proud television owners were offered only fuzzy, blurred, wobbly little pictures transmitted on 1148kHz (medium wave) for just half an hour, from 11am, on certain weekdays.

Viewers were required to have a good memory as well as an excellent imagination in order to follow anything on the flickering 30-line screen: sound came first, then the pictures in alternate blocks of about eight minutes, as both could not be transmitted on a single frequency.

The mechanical process in use in 1930 was invented by the eccentric Scotsman, John Logie Baird. The receiver was a nightmarish Heath Robinson device using a large and dangerous-looking disc whirling round at great speed, and magnifying lenses to make the picture appear at least the size of a cigarette pack.

Since he first demonstrated television to the press in 1926, Baird had been battling with the Post Office and the BBC to be allowed to transmit his pictures in order to carry on his main business of manufacturing and selling the television sets that would receive them.

But all manner of obstacles were placed in Baird's way. One of these was John Reith, a fellow Scot who was the first Director-General of the BBC, itself a mere eight years old when our story begins. Reith mistrusted the whole notion of television (and continued to do so well into his old age) and the BBC engineers rightly thought that Baird's pictures were inadequate for any kind of proper public service television.

As far back as 1908 the eminent scientist, A. A. Campbell Swinton had theorised that the only way to make television work was to use an all-electronic system based on the cathode ray tube. Unfortunately, Swinton also thought that

The control room at Portland Place

the idea would take too much money and effort to bring to practicality.

But when he saw the results of Baird's work he was moved to write in *The Times* in 1928 that "moving images ... approximating in quality to the cinematograph ... are beyond the possible capacity of any mechanism with moving parts ... the only way it can ever he accomplished is by using the vastly superior agency of electrons." Privately, Campbell Swinton expressed the view that Baird and his associates were "rogues, clever rogues and quite unscrupulous, who are fleecing the ignorant public."

Early in 1930, the BBC introduced its revolutionary National and Regional scheme for radio, which meant that they now had more medium wave transmitters at their disposal. Reluctantly, half an hour a day on both the London and Midland Regional wavelengths was handed over to Baird, and so what we might today consider the first television programmes, with synchronised sound and vision, were first shown at the end of March 1930.

Sydney Moseley (Baird's business manager) lost the intended star of the show, Cicely Courtnidge, after telling her that her song was "too twaddish for broadcasting." Her replacement, Gracie Fields, described the studio as "as big as the smallest telephone kiosk."

Performers had to stand, sing, dance or whatever in his 'telephone kiosk' studio in a darkness that was punctured only by the flickering light providing the scanning spot that was reflected back to photocells. And in order that the system could reproduce their features in recognisably human form, artists had to wear bizarre make-up, with pure white faces, black around the lips and sides of the nose, and silver eyelids and lashes.

While Moseley played the impresario, giving himself the title of 'Director of Television Programmes', Baird was busy bolting additional elements to his invention: large screen television using thousands of light bulbs; rotating mirrors rather than discs with holes in them; 'zone television' with the pictures from three cameras joined imperfectly together to create a widescreen image. More importantly, in 1932 Baird was given permission to experiment with what were then called 'ultra-short-waves' on a frequency of 41.09MHz. At the time he was unaware of the BBC's own similar experiments which predated his by a year.

At the same time research engineers, W. F. Tedham and J. D. McGee, behind the backs of their EMI bosses, produced a working cathode ray tube. Officially, EMI were promoting their own mechanical system, but it was only when the BBC turned it down that they started to develop Tedham and McGee's prototype.

The BBC, too, recognised the need to become more involved with the new television and, in August 1932, took over responsibility for the production of the 30-line medium-wave programmes from their own television studio in Broadcasting House, London.

In charge of EMI's research and development

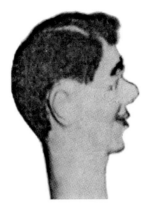

Stooky Bill: **the first 'face' to be televised**

was Alan Blumein – described by those who worked with him as a 'real genius' who understood all aspects of television from vacuum physics to transmitters and studio design. In early 1934 he was able to show the company chairman a satisfactory working prototype which, although giving inferior pictures to those from EMI's own mechanical system, clearly had a far greater development potential.

When the BBC saw the system working in the spring, it was impressed. EMI were impressed enough to join forces with transmitter giants, Marconi to form a new company, Marconi-EMI, with the aim of winning both the receiver and the transmitter business.

Baird xenophobically objected that 27 per cent of the company was controlled by Americans, but that didn't make his pictures any less flickery. So in desperation, Baird came up with his 'intermediate film process' which involved filming the studio action, processing and developing it, and running it through a telecine machine (the only part of the Baird system that could produce worthwhile pictures) at 180 lines.

This process took a mere 54 seconds from start to finish, but relied on a ghastly combination of whirling and grinding mechanics and baths of cyanide and water!

With Baird and Marconi-EMI both claiming 'high definition' television, the time came for a decision on a full scale television service. In the summer of 1934 the government appointed a committee of inquiry, chaired by Lord Selsdon, Postmaster-General in 1922 when BBC radio was established.

Marconi-EMI were still experimenting with a 240-line mechanical system. Isaac Shoenberg, their director of Patent Development and Research Laboratories, single-handedly made the decision that the company would abandon any mechanics and offer Selsdon all-electronic, 405-line television. In one weekend Blumein and his colleagues created the detailed design and specifications of the system that was to survive for some 50 years.

Selsdon gave the BBC 18 months to establish a high-definition television service. Baird's 240-line system and Marconi-EMI's 405-line system were to be

Douglas Birkinshaw,
the first BBC TV Chief Engineer at Ally Pally

tried out on alternate weeks for the first six months. 30-line was abandoned.

Part of Alexandra Palace in north London was leased, and Douglas Birkinshaw, Engineer-in-Charge of television, was given the task of building Britain's first television station which initially had to house studios for both Baird's intermediate film process, Baird's 'spotlight system' (a 240-line version of his 30-line system to be used for continuity announcements only), and the Marconi-EMI studio which was just 2,100 feet square and 25 feet high.

And, of course, a transmitting mast was necessary to carry the 'ultra-shortwave' aerial that was to radiate 17 kilowatts effective power with vision on 45MHz and sound on 41.5MHz. It was perched on top of the south-east tower of the palace originally built as an entertainment venue in 1875.

Director of the Television Service was Gerald Cock. Formerly the BBC's first director of radio OBs, he had been a prospector and miner in the USA, an expert on explosives, had managed a Hollywood film company, and owned a ranch – not your average BBC executive.

Cock assembled his staff on 17 August 1936, saying "I know nothing about television – none of you do, but you've got about four months to think, find out, see what the cameras can do. I suggest you all pile yourselves into cars and go out to see your offices at Alexandra Palace."

When they reached 'Ally Pally' (as Gracie Fields christened it) the sole object in programme planner Cecil Madden's new office – the telephone – was ringing.

**Gerald Cock:
first Director of BBC Television**

It was Cock. "Ah Cecil. Glad I caught you. Wash out everything I said earlier. Radio Show at Olympia has been a great failure – they can't sell stands. They think television can save them and I've agreed. Don't muck about. You're the senior man. Get hold of your staff and ring me back about five o'clock and tell me what you're going to do. This means programmes in about nine days time."

At precisely twelve noon on Wednesday August 26, 1936, BBC Television was on the air and 6,000 visitors to RadiOlympia crowded round the sets on display. The opening variety show was titled *Here's Looking At You*. The name was thought up by Ronnie Hill who had been commissioned to write a new song for the launch. Madden liked the title and built the show around it. With a budget of £300 for artists who were asked to perform live twice

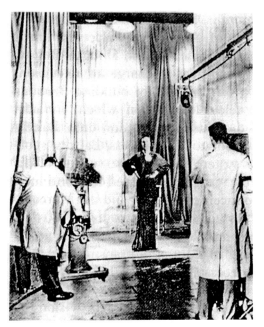

Here's Looking At You:
Miss Elizabeth Cowell
in the announcing position

daily for ten days, the show starred singer Helen McKay (fee £42), two tap dancers, a three-man vocal group, a pantomime horse – and the BBC Television Orchestra.

Only McKay appeared in the first Baird transmission. Baird's Intermediate Film Process was neither ready nor reliable. From this moment it was doomed. But both systems were used to transmit the official opening of the BBC Television Service on November 2, and the service was broadcast for two hours a day, 3-4pm and 9-10pm, except Sundays when, in true Reithian tradition, there were no transmissions until 1938.

The programmes were as varied as the technology would allow. Cookery, ballet, keep fit, current affairs, opera, plays, variety – anything and everything that could be persuaded to travel up the hill to Ally Pally was paraded in front of the cameras. Depending on which week it was, it would mean either the Marconi-EMI cameras (no viewfinders – the scientists hadn't thought of that – and an 8-second dissolve as the only means of cutting between shots), or the

1937 HMV Model 902
TV/Radiogram
List price £126.
Only eleven examples are
thought to have been
manufactured.

motionless and unsmiling Intermediate Film Camera. Twenty minutes of film in the magazine and that was your lot; lens changes done live with blurred and wobbly bits in between; constant contrast changes, and air bubbles in the developed film which also meant gurgling noises on the optical soundtrack.

A fire at the Baird Television headquarters at Crystal Palace a few weeks later destroyed all the spares and it was a foregone conclusion that the Baird system, cyanide and all, would be abandoned at the first possible opportunity. The axe fell in February 1937.

In May of that year the coronation of King George VI was the first real television outside broadcast – and with an estimated 50,000 viewers it was to contribute much to the sales and popularity of pre-war TV, even though cameras weren't allowed into Westminster Abbey and had to be content with pictures of the arrivals and departures of state coaches.

With the departure of Baird's equipment BBC Television was now able to use two studios at Alexandra Palace, which made a difference to the logistics of running a television station without the benefit of videotape. Filmed items were usually scheduled between live programmes to allow five or ten minutes for the setting up of the next live programme. There was no BBC news service, but the British Movietone News and the Gaumont-British News cinema newsreels were shown each day, one in the afternoon and one in the evening on an alternating basis.

Much of what we now take for granted in terms of television technique was developed between 1936 and 1939. With no precedents anywhere in the world the BBC Television team (220 in 1936, 500 by 1939) broke new ground every day. They televised the FA Cup Final, Wimbledon, the Derby, Test Match cricket. They showed comedy series, thriller serials, costume drama and quiz games.

Alas, practically none of it survives. No satisfactory method of recording the output had yet been developed, and what few fragments remain were re-creations of televised items that were taken to a film studio and shot on celluloid for inclusion in the daily demonstration film, shown at 11am for the benefit of television dealers.

20,000 sets had been sold by 1939. There were some 100,000 viewers living within range of the sole transmitter in London, and the BBC had plans to build another in the north of England.

At just past noon on September 1, 1939, after an extra unscheduled Mickey Mouse cartoon, the announcer trailed the afternoon's Mantovani programme and a later Galsworthy play, and bade viewers good afternoon. Twenty minutes of test pattern and tone followed. Ally Pally then fell silent for the duration of the Second World War.

Significant dates 1930-39

31 Mar 1930 First transmission of 30-line television with synchronised sound.

3 Jun 1931 Derby pictures transmitted for the first time.

19 Aug 1931 First BBC programme televised from Studio 10 at Waterloo Bridge.

15 Oct 1931 Simulcast of Jack Payne radio programme from Savoy Hill.

22 Aug 1932 BBC takes over production of 30-line programmes.

29 Jan 1934 First demonstration of all-electric TV to EMI chairman.

16 May 1934 Selsdon Committee set up to investigate feasibility of launching a public television service.

31 Jan 1935 Selsdon recommends BBC start high definition service by July 1936 using Baird and Marconi-EMI systems.

5 Feb 1935 First meeting of the Television Advisory Committee.

1 Jun 1935 BBC's 21 year lease on Alexandra Palace begins.

11 Sep 1935 BBC closes 30-line service.

12 Aug 1936 First high definition test transmission.

2 Nov 1936 High definition service officially begins.

30 Nov 1936 Crystal Palace fire destroys Baird's offices and workshops.

6 Feb 1937	Baird 240-line transmissions discontinued.
12 May 1937	Coronation of King George VI: first BBC TV Outside Broadcast.
1 Sep 1939	Television service closed down "for reasons of national defence".

Prominent People 1930-1939

A. A. Campbell Swinton — First to propose system of electronic TV, 1908.

John Logie Baird — First man to publicly demonstrate television, Apr 1925.

Karl Braun — Inventor of the cathode ray tube, 1897.

Boris Rosing — Proposed TV system using cathode ray tube, 1907.

V. K. Zworykin — Rosing's pupil, who patented electronic system in 1923.

Harold Bradly — First television producer, in charge of Baird programmes from 1931.

Tony Bridgewater — Baird engineer 1928-32, BBC Senior studio engineer 1936; responsible for Coronation coverage, 1937.

E. Robb – BBC's only 30-line TV producer.

Alan Blumein — EMI's 'genius' who created detailed spec. for 405-line television system.

D.C. Birkinshaw — First Chief Television Engineer at the BBC, 1932; responsible for setting up Alexandra Palace, 1936.

Gerald Cock — First BBC Director of Television.

Cecil Madden — BBC TV programme planner and producer, responsible for putting together the first television schedules and producing the first programmes.

Cecil Lewis — Talks Producer.

George More O'Ferrall — Drama Producer.

Stephen Thomas — Music Producer.

Dallas Bower — Opera and film.

Mary Adams — First woman producer (replaced Lewis in 1937).

Philip Dorté — First OB producer.

Desmond Campbell — Ex-professional photographer turned shift engineer. He was the only man who knew about lighting, and ended up as the first Lighting Engineer. Described by Birkinshaw as 'Father of television lighting'.

Mary Allen — First Head of Wardrobe and Make-up.

Peter Bax — First Head of Design.

L. Marsland Gander — First television critic, of the *Daily Telegraph.*

Sydney Mosely — Baird's business manager, and first announcer on the 30-line service.

Leslie Mitchell — First announcer on the high definition service.

Elizabeth Cowell — First woman announcer.

Radio Times **special 'Television' edition – Oct 23, 1936**

Key Programmes 1930-39

The Man With The Flower In His Mouth — Pirandello's play was the first to be televised (in Britain) on 14 July 1930. The BBC producer was Lance Sieveking – the cast included Gladys Young, Lionel Millard and Earle Gray in the title role.

Derby (1931) — First 30-line OB. Viewers saw the horses pass the winning post.

Here's Looking At You (26 Aug 1936) — First high definition programme from Alexandra Palace, shown twice daily to RadiOlympia visitors. Variety show starred The Three Admirals, Miss Lutie and her Wonder Horse 'Pogo'. Leslie Mitchell introduced the first edition; Elizabeth Cowell joined him for later programmes. Producer: Cecil Madden.

Variety (2 Nov 1936) — Official opening show, with dancers Buck and Bubbles, jugglers the Lai Founs, singer Adele Dixon and the Television Orchestra playing Eric Coates' Television March. Producer: Cecil Madden.

Picture Page (8 Oct 1936 onwards) — First topical magazine programme. Presented by Canadian actress Joan Miller who sat at a switchboard and 'connected' viewers to the programme's items. She was the first true TV 'star'. Producer: George More O'Ferrall. Editor: Cecil Madden.

Television Comes To London (2 Nov 1936) — The BBC's first filmed documentary. Directors: Bill Barbrook and Dallas Bower.

Mickey Mouse — Walt Disney provided the BBC with two cartoons a day.

Marigold (5 Nov 1936) — First play on high definition, 'scenes from' Scottish comedy by L. Allen Harker and F. R. Pryor. Sophie Stewart starred, George More O'Ferrall directed.

Ann and Harold [Aug 26, 1936]— First serial, a five-part romantic comedy. Starred Ann Todd.

Episode One: *Ann and Harold*

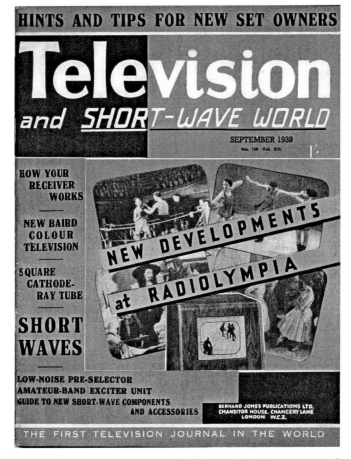

The last issue of the world's first television magazine prior to World War II – September 1939

Percy Ponsonby's Progress — First comedy series, with Charles Hyslop.

The Coronation (12 May 1937) — First true outside broadcast. Producer: Tony Bridgewater. Commentator: Freddie Grisewood. Estimated 50,000 viewers.

Remembrance Day Service (11 Nov 1937) — First OB of this annual event. Producer: Philip Dorté.

Chamberlain Arrives At Heston (13 Sep 1938) — OB coverage of Neville Chamberlain's return from visiting Hitler.

II
Back for Good This Time
The 40s

Post-war television:
the key political and programming moves

If things didn't look too bright for television when the 30s began, they looked positively black at the dawn of the following decade. The war had brought television to an abrupt halt, mainly because of fears that the high-power VHF signal from Alexandra Palace could be used as the perfect tracking beacon for enemy aircraft on bombing missions.

The transmitter was switched on during the war when it was discovered that the Germans were using a radar-based device which allowed planes to establish their exact location. By receiving these radar signals and retransmitting them from Muswell Hill, the system was confused; the false locations thus relayed to the German pilots shattered their confidence in the system.

But it was clear that when the war ended a decision would have to be taken on the future of British television. There had been suggestions at the outbreak that perhaps the cinema industry might operate its own closed-circuit service. Later the idea was floated that cinema interests might replace the BBC.

The inevitable result was the setting-up of a Committee of Inquiry, led by Lord Hankey. It was established in secret in September 1943, and the public only became aware of its deliberations in January 1944. After receiving evidence from a variety of sources with all manner of proposed changes, including the acceptance of advertising and sponsorship, the Hankey Committee concluded, in March 1945, that "television is here to stay – and that it should continue on much the same basis as before, with the BBC resuming the 405-line service from Alexandra Palace, London, as soon as possible. The London programme was to be extended to "six centres of populous districts outside London" whenever practicable. The committee believed this was necessary "to drive receiver prices down".

Seven months later, on 9 October 1945, the Labour government accepted

**The enduring *Muffin The Mule* chats to *Annette Mills*
while *Ann Hogarth* pulls the strings**

Hankey's recommendations, and the BBC immediately set about relaunching television. By February 1946 test transmissions were on the air, and staff in place at Alexandra Palace.

They were led by Maurice Gorham, the dynamic former editor of *Radio Times,* whose latter war years had been spent setting-up and running the joint

British/US/Canadian radio network, 'The AEF Programme', which introduced many of the programming innovations that nowadays would be considered the bedrock of BBC radio.

Immediately after the war Gorham had been architect and first Head of the Light Programme. But Sir William Haley, then Director-General of the Corporation, knew that Gorham's dream had always been of television. As pre-war editor of *Radio Times* he'd already had the opportunity to see the potential of the service and, after a mere five months at the 'Light', Gorham was given the chance to make his dream come true, as Head of Television Service, earning £2,000 a year.

As servicemen returned to civilian life many of those originally associated with the pre-war television service made their way back up Muswell Hill to the Palace – which in 1939 had been abandoned, *Marie Celeste* style, with cups of tea left unconsumed in offices.

But Gorham and his team showered the Sleeping Beauty with kisses and soon the cramped building was buzzing with activity. One of the first tasks was to produce the demonstration film which was to be screened every morning at 11am for the benefit of the retail trade. This was shot on film and Philip Dorté directed the assortment of what were presented to viewers as 'clips from programmes'. In fact, they were re-creations filmed in advance of the re-opening, as telerecording was impossible in 1946.

Gorham had chosen as his right-hand man, fellow Irishman, Denis Johnston, a playwright who for many years had been producer at Dublin's Abbey Theatre. Johnston had film work and was unable to take up the job straightaway, so the task of planning the re-opening programme, and the first programme schedule, fell once again to Cecil Madden. Even after Johnston's arrival, the planning and production of variety programmes was left to Madden, whose contacts in the showbiz world were second to none.

As plans were made to relaunch the service, two problems were uppermost in Gorham's mind. One was the budget. Television was allowed to spend a mere £249,140 on operating costs in 1946-7 – less than in 1939, when costs had been far lower. Capital expenditure on equipment in the first year was just £14,487 compared with radio's £214,587. The following year (1947-8) the BBC spent a total of £716,666 on its fledgling visual service, and a massive £6,556,293 on the senior sound service.

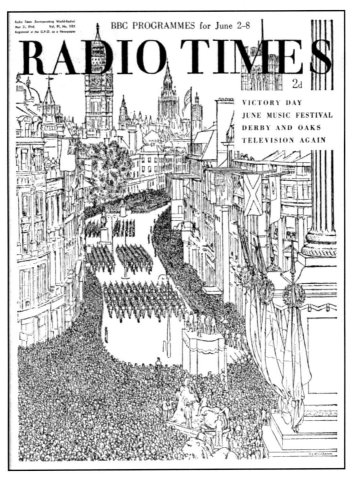

Victory Day *Radio Times* – May 31, 1946

These figures were largely justified by the small numbers of viewers – in 1947 there were just 14,560 television licence holders. But Gorham's other problem was linked to the size of the budget – the attitude of the management at Broadcasting House.

Television was very much the poor relation of radio. Although various noises were made about "allowing television its freedom to develop", there were many within the BBC – including Haley – who were afraid of the television monster they were about to unleash. They worried that it would take over people's homes and lives, and feared most that the major casualty would be sound broadcasting.

So although Gorham was Head of Television Service (with the internal status of a Controller) he was responsible for just over half the people who worked at Alexandra Palace. Setting aside catering and house staff, and registry clerks (who belonged to Secretariat), the main body was composed of engineers, who were part of the Operations and Maintenance department of the BBC's Engineering Division.

Thus Douglas Birkinshaw – the senior engineer in television – had five layers of management between himself and the Director-General, and this acted as a considerable restraint on his, and Gorham's ability to develop the service.

Space was a problem too. The original EMI studio A was augmented by studio B – originally the Baird studio – but this still somehow, according to Gorham, "retained its air of defeat and failure", with only three cameras (as opposed to the four in studio A), a cramped gallery that projected into the middle, and racks which were squeezed into an alley. The synonym for a show that could be given no resources worth speaking of was that it would have to go into "the wrong end of B".

The date for the resumption of programmes was dictated by circumstances. The service had to be up and running by June 8 in order to televise the Victory Day celebrations, but it would not be possible to pull together the resources to televise the Derby on June 6. So June 7 chose itself as relaunch day.

A decision was taken to emphasise continuity with the service of the 30s. The programmes therefore included a repeat of the Mickey Mouse cartoon which had closed the service, and Mantovani and his Orchestra – scheduled to be seen at 3.35pm on 1 September 1939 – appeared at 3.35 on 7 June 1946. Likewise Harry Rutherford's *Cabaret Cartoons* programme (which Cecil Madden produced) scheduled to kick off the evening of Saturday 2 September 1939, eventually kicked off the evening of Saturday 8 June 1946, complete with Levanda (foot juggler) as promised seven years earlier.

At three o'clock precisely, Jasmine Bligh greeted those viewers whose sets had survived the war, with the words "Remember me?" – and the Postmaster-General made the inevitable speech. Margot Fonteyn danced, and David Low (creator of 'Colonel Blimp') chatted to the cameras whilst drawing. George More O'Ferrall's production of *The Dark Lady of the Sonnets* concluded the first afternoon's bill of fare. It must have been the most over-rehearsed of

1948 – *Mary Malcolm* faces the cameras as a new TV announcer

television dramas, as it was used as a practice vehicle for training technicians long after the cast could recite their lines in their sleep.

The triumph of the relaunch was the outside broadcast coverage of the Victory Parade, with Freddie Grisewood and Richard Dimbleby as commentators. The press enthused about the clarity of the pictures. Winston Churchill's cufflinks and Clement Atlee's moustache could clearly be seen, they gushed.

Astonishingly, there were no breakdowns. Although the vision circuit from London's West End to Ally Pally had lain dormant since 1939, like everything else in the nation, it all worked perfectly.

But only the handful of viewers in London were able to enjoy the spectacle. The six additional transmitters to service main centres of population outside the capital, recommended by the Hankey Committee, had yet to be constructed; Britain's economy was in no fit state to take on major public sector capital spending. Robert Barr's radio documentary '*Television is Here Again*', in the Home Service, was the closest the rest of the country would get to the new medium for many years to come.

Restrictions on materials and labour meant that a supply of new television sets was not as forthcoming as the Television Advisory Committee had predicted. Their estimates of half a million sets by the end of 1948 was well off beam: a mere 134,000 sets were in use then and those included pre-war receivers.

Watching Television in 1949   *by Lynda Waller*

This served to make television a rare commodity, and thus all the more desirable. The London *Evening News* commented in 1948 that "the television aerial has become the symbol of social superiority down our street" – and watching television became a communal habit, with crowds of friends and neighbours nightly cramming the sitting-rooms of those lucky enough to possess a set.

Transmission times remained almost as limited as before the war. Apart from the hour-long demonstration film in the morning, there was an hour of programmes between 3 and 4 in the afternoon, and evening programmes began at 8.30pm and ended with the News (in sound only) at l0pm. Outside broadcasts were allowed to extend beyond these times: in its first full week back on air BBC Television added three extra hours' coverage of The Wightman Cup tennis from Wimbledon.

Perhaps the greatest triumph for immediate post-war OBs was coverage of the 1948 Olympic Games, held in England. Before the Games Ian Orr-Ewing warned viewers against overkill: "From correspondence received, it is clear that a large percentage of viewers still try to see all the programmes televised. It is hoped that this habit will not persist during the Olympic Games or viewers will be easily recognised in the streets of London by their pallid appearance!"

The BBC was acutely aware that this was to be the first international showcase for British television, and manufacturers drew lots to see who would be allowed to install free sets in embassies, legations and the chief games centres.

In one week, there were 17.5 hours of live coverage, 11.25 hours of which were outside normal transmission times.

Although television was proving an immediate success with the public, behind the scenes all was not well. Gorham resisted organisational changes that further diluted the autonomy of his position, and resigned "full of despair" in November 1947 when Haley tried to move him back to the Light Programme. His replacement was Norman Collins, who had ironically been his successor at the Light Programme, and who was willing to take the job under new conditions.

Collins was perceived as an enthusiast for the BBC Television Service. He was very much an enthusiast for television – but not necessarily for the BBC.

Soon after taking over from Gorham, Collins discovered how badly overworked practically everybody at Alexandra Palace was. Equally, the space allotted was quite inadequate. But Collins kept up the pressure on those above him. In the end the BBC committed themselves in 1948 to a programme of expansion throughout the country, and to the purchase of new studios in Shepherd's Bush. In 1949 the BBC bought a 13.5 acre site at White City in west London, and began to draw up plans for a massive new purpose-built Television Centre. It was to be 11 years before it was operational.

As the decade ended, an unexpected opportunity arose for the BBC to acquire additional premises. After a nail-biting weekend of personal telephone calls between Collins and the governors at their homes, BBC Television took possession of the five studios at Shepherd's Bush formerly owned by The Rank Organisation.

Meanwhile the creative teams worked on, constantly discovering and inventing new techniques and finding ways to compensate for the many 'bans' that faced post-war TV. No films (because the Renters, Exhibitors and Producers – REP – joint committee would not allow any material they controlled to be screened for fear of losing cinema audiences); no West End theatre shows (managers had banned those on the same grounds as the REP); the major music-hall circuits (Stoll, Moss and GTC) would not allow any of their acts to appear; the British Boxing Board of Control forbade their bouts being televised; the Epsom Grandstand Association would not allow the Derby to be shown; the Football League kept their matches to themselves; even Chappells, the music publishers, placed serious restrictions on the music that BBC Television could play.

Gorham, and the Governors were – in the genteel parlance of the decade – "startled" by this list. "I began to wonder where we did get our programmes from," said Gorham.

The BBC started shooting their own Television Newsreel in 1948: one 15-minute film a week at first, but by the end of 1949 there were two editions, each repeated. Although West End theatres wouldn't allow the cameras in, there were others which would, and did. If top UK performers couldn't appear, their continental cousins could – and a string of 'Euro-cabaret' shows were created to accommodate them. Amateur boxing was screened; other racecourses welcomed the BBC's cameras; Rugby Football gained a new audience; and other music publishers were only too willing to have their tunes played on 'T/V'.

The 40s ended with probably the most important event of all: the Sutton Coldfield transmitter, near Birmingham, came into service 15 days before the decade ended. It was the most powerful television transmitter in the world, with its aerial placed on the highest transmitter mast. It brought television to millions of new viewers inside its official service area, from Mansfield in the north, to Cheltenham in the south; and with a little help from high masts and powerful aerials, to viewers in the north country, Wales and the Severn area, albeit sometimes through a curtain of snow.

Plans were afoot to extend the transmitter network in the early 50s, and with new studios and greater finances, BBC Television was at last more comfortable. Although a Committee of Inquiry into the Future of Broadcasting had been set up under Lord Beveridge in July, there was no reason to suppose that BBC Television did not have a rosy future.

1949 ended with a performance of *Toad of Toad Hall*, "For Older Children", and a screening of ancient cinema serial '*Custer's Last Stand*' for the younger ones; Jack Hulbert in a specially written version of the pantomime *Dick Whittington*; and the return of Leslie Mitchell as interviewer on *Picture Page*.

Significant Dates 1940-49

Sep 1943	Hankey Committee appointed to consider the re-instatement and development of the TV service.
9 Oct 1945	Government accepts Hankey proposals.
2 Nov 1945	Maurice Gorham appointed Head of Television Service.
Feb 1946	Test transmissions begin
7 Jun 1946	BBC Television service from Alexandra Palace resumed.
8 Jun 1946	Victory Day Parade.
10 Feb 1947	Television suspended during national fuel crisis. Resumed on 11 March.
20 Nov 1947	Royal Wedding televised, first use of new CPS Emitron cameras.
5 Jan 1948	First BBC Newsreel.
24 Aug 1948	Government announces approval of BBC plans to build new television transmitters throughout the UK.
21 Jun 1949	Lord Beveridge appointed Chairman of Committee on the Future of Broadcasting.
29 Jul 1949	First TV weather forecast.

Prominent People 1940-49

Maurice Gorham — First post-war Head of Television Service. Former editor of *Radio Times*. Set up the wartime AEF Programme and then the peacetime Light Programme. Resigned in November 1947.

Norman Collins — Gorham's replacement, former Light Programme Head.

Denis Johnston — Programme Director and Deputy Head of Television. Irish playwright and pre-war producer of *Picture Page*.

Cecil McGivern — Television Programme Director from March 1947, described by TV critic Peter Black as 'The true architect of BBC Television'. Briefly joined Rank Organisation before coming to TV at the age of 40.

Douglas Birkinshaw — Superintendent Engineer (television) resumed his pre-war role as television's Chief Engineer.

Cecil Madden — Programme Organiser who was responsible for the first resumed programming and planning, and under Johnston remained responsible for variety and planning.

Pat Hillyard — First Presentation Director, taking over as Head of Light Entertainment in December 1947.

George More O'Ferrall — Senior Producer (drama) – won the Television Society's first Oscar award for 1947 for his production of 'Hamlet'.

Mary Adams — Senior Producer (talks).

Grace Wyndham-Goldie — Television Talks Producer in 1948, went on to be one of the most influential producers of all time.

Peter Bax — Design Manager, former a.s.m at Drury Lane.

Harold Cox — First Newsreel Manager, formerly with Gaumont British News, and assistant TV OB manager before the war.

Jasmine Bligh — Briefly resumed her pre-war role as lady announcer.

Winifred Shotter — Announcer from 1946.

McDonald Hobley — Announcer from 1946.

Sylvia Peters — Announcer from 1947

Richard Dimbleby — Commentator.

Richard Hearne (aka 'Mr Pastry') — Comedy actor making his first appearance on 19 August 1946.

Eric Robinson — Conductor of the television orchestra.

Mr Pastry aka Richard Hearne

Key Programmes 1940-49

The Silence of the Sea (7 Jun 1946) — First full-length post-war drama, starred Kenneth More.

The Victory Parade (8 Jun 1946) — First post-war OB, with Freddie Grisewood and Richard Dimbleby as commentators.

For the Children (9 Jun 1946 onwards) — At first this was a mere half-hour on Sunday afternoon, with Ann Hogarth's puppets and a conjuror. It soon filled a whole hour and introduced children to ...

Muffin the Mule (20 Oct 1946 onwards) — Annette Mills presented, played piano, sang songs and generally acted as a long-suffering foil to Ann Hogarth's exuberant string puppet.

In Our Garden (9 Jun 1946 onwards) — Fred Streeter's weekly visit to the TV garden in the grounds of Ally Pally.

Philip Harben – the first tv cook

Cookery (from 12 Jun 1946) — One of television's singular creations which introduced Philip Harben as the television chef, on 1 Sep 1947.

Demonstration Film (daily from 17 Jun 1946) — For many this was their first glimpse of television. A frequently updated mixture of programme clips, restaged for film cameras, and bursts of Test Card shown every weekday morning between 11am and noon. Produced by Marcus Cooper, directed by Philip Dorté.

Kaleidoscope (1946 onwards) — A magazine programme that mixed games and competitions with studio interviews and 'expert' demonstrations. McDonald Hobley presented. Leslie Welch was 'The Memory Man' and Ronnie Waldham presented his 'Puzzle Corner'.

Television Newsreel (5 Jan 1948 onwards) — BBC's first TV news service, initially once a week, then twice, eventually daily. It was modelled on cinema newsreels.

SOBELL Table Model T90

Designed for Women (from 6 Nov 1947) — First example of 'daytime TV' genre, with Jeanne Heal presenting a mixture of women's features.

Report on Germany (9 May 1948) — First full-length (45 mins) documentary film, produced by Robert Barr using German camera crews directed by G. del Strother.

Olympic Games (from 29 Jul 1948) — BBC's first TV coverage of the Olympics was only possible because in 1948 they were held in London! Richard Dimbleby was commentator for the Opening Ceremony which was performed by the King.

Rooftop Rendezvous, Café Continental, & Casa D'Esalta — Assorted nightclubs all created in the Ally Pally studios as vehicles for a variety of European cabaret acts.

Inventors' Club (from 6 Apr 1948) — A monthly programme in which the best inventions were appraised by Geoffrey Boumphrey, and presented by Leslie Harden.

Family Affair (from 29 October 1949) — First serial, about a fictional family, The Connovers – Linda and Henry, Marion, Tony, Bunty, Martin and Maggie the cook – scripted by Eric Maschwitz from an idea by Betty Farmer. Michael Mills was producer.

III
A Growing Concern
The 50's
'Classic' TV
and the setting up of ITV

On 1 January 1950, a total of 3.75 hours were broadcast by BBC Television from two transmitters with a combined power of 134kW to some 340,000 licence holders. On 31 December 1959, BBC and ITV provided nearly 10.5 million licence holders with 17.5 hours of programmes from 33 transmitters with a power of over 2,617kW. This was the decade when television grew up.

An early panel game success for BBC TV (1951)

As the 50s got underway the single BBC Television channel seemed likely to remain unchanged. The Beveridge Committee – appointed in 1949 to look into the future of broadcasting – had come down emphatically against what it called 'sponsored television' since it believed that advertisers would dictate programme content as they did in the USA. But there were voices of dissent.

Tory MP Selwyn Lloyd – then Foreign Affairs Minister, and a member of the Beveridge Committee – issued his own report suggesting that it was unacceptable for the BBC to hold on to "the brute force of monopoly" and that a British Television Corporation be established with the right to accept sponsored programmes and advertising.

Although the members of the Beveridge Committee appeared to have equated "sponsorship" with "commercial", the fine print of their 500-page, 100-recommendation tome suggests that they were aware of the subtle differences between sponsorship and spot advertising. Indeed, three of the Committee also suggested that a public service broadcasting corporation could allow a limited amount of time for spot "commercials".

In July 1951 the Labour Government, having accepted the principal recommendations of Beveridge, fell in November of that year. The incumbent Conservative Government decided to follow Selwyn Lloyd's route, and rushed out a White Paper that favoured "some element of competition", causing apoplexy in many establishment circles. "Somebody introduced Christianity into England. And somebody introduced smallpox, bubonic plague and the Black Death. Somebody is minded now to introduce sponsored broadcasting," spluttered former BBC Director-General Lord Reith in the Lords.

Things weren't so hunky-dory at Ally Pally either. Controller of Television, Norman Collins, had resigned in October 1950 when former Third Programme Controller, George Barnes, was appointed over his head as Director of Television. Collins perceived this as a clear sign of the BBC's "vested interest in sound broadcasting" and promptly contacted the Conservative Party to see what role he might play in the creation of commercial TV.

"If we hadn't fired Collins there would be no commercial television now," was the later judgement of Lord Simon of Wythenshawe, BBC Chairman at the time. Certainly, Collins devoted much energy and effort to the project: he formed an alliance with C. O. Stanley of equipment manufacturers, Pye Ltd, and the influential industrialist, Sir Robert Renwick.

This triumvirate set up the Popular Television Association as a counter to the anti-commercial National Television Council, which had several distinguished elder statesmen on board. The NTC had set about a publicity campaign to persuade the great British public that commercial television was at least akin to the Black Death.

TV announcer *Sylvia Peters*
TV Mirror February 20th, 1954

While the politicians, businessmen and entrepreneurs were embroiled in these machinations, whither BBC Television? For much of the public, television began with the Coronation. On 2 June 1953, Queen Elizabeth II was the first monarch to be truly crowned "in sight of all the people". The television outside broadcast was the most ambitious ever undertaken: seven hours non-stop with five cameras inside Westminster Abbey, and 21 at five sites outside; a year in the planning. 'Lobby' – Seymour de Lotbiniere – was in charge for a second time (having masterminded the much less ambitious three-camera coverage in 1937), and Peter Dimmock produced the programme, which was viewed by a record-breaking UK audience in excess of 20 million.

Although the formal Eurovision network was still a year away a radio link across the channel allowed the Coronation to be seen live in France, Germany, Italy and Holland; and film recordings of the TV coverage were flown out to North America and Japan.

US networks NBC and CBS vied to get pictures on-air first. CBS succeeded in Boston at 4.26pm. The RAF flew film of the BBC coverage to Canada, where CBC relayed

1953 Coronation *Radio Times*

pictures from Montreal to Buffalo, New York for ABC and NBC to re-broadcast. Some 85 million people watched in the USA.

The Coronation had been the carrot, but continued improvements in range, quality and quantity of BBC Television programmes were appreciated by an increasing army of viewers, and once ITV spread forth of London, sound broadcasting was relegated to minority audience status.

In July 1954 the Television Act received Royal Assent, and a few days later the Independent Television Authority held its first meeting.

Chairing the new body was Arts Council chairman, Sir Kenneth Clark, who had been Controller of Home Publicity in the wartime propaganda Ministry of Information. The former head of publications in the same Ministry, Robert Fraser, was appointed Director-General of the ITA. Fraser, an Australian who had studied at the socialist-dominated London School of Economics before becoming leader writer at the *Daily Herald*, was persuaded by Norman Collins to move from a cosy job in charge of the Central Office of Information.

Urgent priority was given to the advertisement of the first licences, which was made within a few weeks of the first meeting. The Authority members were all chosen by the Postmaster-General, the then government figure in charge of broadcasting matters. The ITA was given all the powers it needed to make decisions unfettered by Government. After interviewing the various applicant groups for the London, Midlands and Northern franchise areas, and considering its brief to create competition in the supply of programming, the Authority decided to split the licence for each area into a weekday and weekend – and thus awarded licences to four different groups.

Between the licence awards and the start of transmissions there was endless shifting of shareholdings and company control as some of the winners merged with elements of losing groups, and one – the Kemsley Press/Maurice Winnick Group, chosen to serve Midlands and North at weekends – withdrew shortly before ITV was launched in London.

Finally, the Authority and its contractors were content with each other: cable operator Broadcast Relay Services and Associated Newspapers came together to form Associated-Rediffusion (London, weekdays); Incorporated Television Programme Co (led by showbiz entrepreneur Mr Prince Littler) merged with the Collins/Stanley/Renwick Associated Broadcasting Development Co to form what was first called Associated Broadcasting Co and later Associated TeleVision (London, weekends / Midlands, weekdays) with Collins as deputy chairman; Granada Television (formed by Sydney Bernstein's successful Granada Theatres group) was given weekdays in the North (both sides of the Pennines); and at the last minute Associated British Cinemas were given Midlands/North weekends as ABC Television.

When ITV opened on 22 September 1955, it did so with Sir John Barbirolli conducting The Hallé Orchestra's Guildhall performance of Elgar's Overture "Cockaigne" (In London Town) – a tune which remained Associated-Rediffusion's callsign for several years.

The rest of that first evening included a variety show, featuring stars who were to become regular faces on the new Channel 9. It was produced by Bill Ward for the Associated Broadcasting Co. A month later the name was changed

TV TIMES

McDONALD
HOBLEY
SEE PAGE THREE

McDonald Hobley
– announcer from 1946 –
First Northern edition of *TV Times* – May 4, 1956

to Associated Television. There were drama excerpts with Dame Edith Evans, Sir John Gielgud and Alec Guinness; professional boxing from Shoreditch Town Hall; a *Star Cabaret* with Billy Ternent's Orchestra; and a glimpse of some of the guests at ITV's gala opening party at the Mayfair, interviewed by none other than Leslie Mitchell, celebrating his second television opening night.

That first night's viewing was, of course, untypical. The programmes a week later were a better indication of the 'new TV'.

Daytime programmes included a soap, an advertising magazine, a short feature on modern architecture and a sing-song for the over 60s. Children's TV consisted of an old Mickey Rooney cinema serial, a quiz, and a *Hopalong Cassidy* western; and peaktime included a classical piano recital, a panel game featuring Jeremy Thorpe, variety with Flanagan and Allan and The Tiller Girls, a popular play, and a documentary on atomic energy. Plus the weather forecast by Squadron Leader Lawrie West.

The 'alternative programme' spread quickly across the UK. Midlands viewers enjoyed *Robin Hood* on their first night in 1956; Granada wisely billed "No Names – Only a Promise" for their northern opening, which turned out to include *A Tribute To The BBC;* and in 1957 STV offered *This Is Scotland* complete with the suave song-and-dance man Jack Buchanan making what turned out to be his last public appearance.

Much of what was seen on the small, 405-line murky grey-and-white tubes of the 50s is still to be found on today's hi-tech colour screens.

Come Dancing (1950); *Panorama* started in 1953 as a fortnightly topical magazine, moved to its Monday night slot in 1955 with Richard Dimbleby as anchorman; *This Is Your Life* started on the BBC in 1955 with long-time host Eamonn Andrews as first 'subject'; *Take Your Pick* transferred from Radio Luxembourg to ITV in 1955 with 'quiz inquisitor Michael Miles'; *Sooty* was adopted by Harry Corbett (father of Matthew) in 1955.

Granada's *What The Papers Say* launched in 1956, also the year of the first Eurovision Song Contest, which was televised from Lugano in Switzerland. In 1957 a young Patrick Moore began exploring *The Sky At Night.* The following year David Coleman was first put in a studio to link the Saturday afternoon mixture of sports OBs under the banner of

Eamonn Andrews*, complete with book in *This is Your Life

Grandstand; and at 5pm on Thursday 16 October 1958, Christopher Trace and Leila Willliams presented the first of a weekly series for younger viewers that dealt with "toys, model railways, games, stories, cartoons" – it was, of course, *Blue Peter.*

Many other household names made their television debuts in the 50s. On 6 January 1956, BBC screened a live OB from London's Vanbrugh Theatre

Stanley Baxter and **Betty Marsden**
in the BBC's "souffle entertainment" *On the Bright Side*

which presented Finals Students at RADA in Goldsmith's comedy *She Stoops To Conquer.* Among the cast were Albert Finney, Roy Kinnear, Antony Brown and Richard Briers. And the fortnightly revue *On The Bright Side,* shown by the BBC in the summer of 1959, boasted amongst its dancers Amanda Barrie and Una Stubbs. Michael Aspel was a BBC TV announcer, and Des O'Connor was guesting in *The Lonnie Donegan Show*; Roger Moore was *Ivanhoe* on ITV; Honor Blackman was fronting the advertising magazine *TV Beauty Salon,* and Australian singer Lorrae Desmond had her own show on the Beeb, long before going home to star in *A Country Practice.*

Television came into the classroom, too. The BBC had carried out an experiment in May 1952 when it transmitted 20 schools programmes to six schools in Middlesex on a special channel. But it was beaten to a regular broadcast service by Associated-Rediffusion who launched their schools television service on 13 May 1957 with *Looking And Seeing,* a programme which sought to demonstrate to children "how we can use our eyes". The BBC's schools television service began four months later.

The early days of ITV were not, however, plain sailing. Although the majority of viewers clearly chose to watch ITV when given a choice of programme, it took some time to arrive at a well-balanced schedule. When, towards the end of 1955, some of the more highbrow programming was shifted out of peaktime, and the timing and amount of News programmes were altered, there were mutterings about ITV going downmarket.

There was little choice since finances were at a critical level and at the time ITV could easily have collapsed had there not been some changes to the balance of output. The ITA required 'minority' programming to be there – advertisers did not. The Authority wanted high transmitter rentals in order to finance their expansion programme. These were temporarily reduced, and by the time the ITA and programme companies had reached some agreement on their permanent levels, the cash was rolling in thick and fast, prompting the classic on-air remark from Canadian newspaper magnate, Roy Thomson, chairman of Scottish Television, that having an ITV franchise was "just like having a licence to print your own money". It was a light-hearted aside that he, and the whole of ITV would live to often regret.

The vast increase in production during the decade could not, of course, have been sustained from two cramped studios in Alexandra Palace. New studios sprang up across the UK, creating employment and pushing hitherto inexperienced technicians, directors and performers sharply up the learning curve.

The BBC took over the former Rank film studios at Lime Grove, added Riverside studios in Hammersmith, opened a Television Theatre in Shepherd's Bush and regional studios around the country.

Associated-Rediffusion transformed a former Air Ministry building in London's Kingsway into 'Television House' where they had two studios and ITN one. There were four more at Wembley and two others around London. ATV had the use of several major London theatres – including the Palladium – which it was able to utilise with the help of its two OB units. There was a control centre in Foley Street – now the headquarters of the Independent Television Commission – a theatre at Wood Green and film studios at Elstree, Nettlefold and Highbury.

ABC and Southern both converted cinemas into television studios. Anglia turned Norwich's old Agricultural Hall into their headquarters, and Scottish Television similarly transformed Glasgow's Theatre Royal, but had the foresight to retain the stage and decorative plasterwork so that when they left it

A selection of ITV first editions

was restored to its original glory as Glasgow's new Opera House.

ABC and ATV jointly constructed the Alpha Television studios in Birmingham at the former New Theatre at Aston Cross; Granada built its Television Centre in Manchester from scratch; TWW converted an old farmhouse at Pontcanna Fields into Cardiff's first studios; Tyne Tees utilised two Newcastle warehouses; and when Sir Laurence Olivier introduced viewers to Ulster Television on 29 October 1959, he did so from a once derelict Victorian yellow brick building in Belfast's Ormeau Road.

By the end of 1959, television had been transformed. No longer was it an amusing diversion put together by and for a few well-heeled Home Counties sorts: it was the means by which the great mass of the UK received their entertainment, news, sport and information. Television had become an industry.

A typical ITV master control – 1957

Prominent People 1950-59

Norman Collins — Head of BBC Television until 13 October 1950. Took charge of Associated TeleVision in 1954.

George Barnes — BBC's Director of Television from October 1950

Cecil McGivern — BBC Controller of Television Programmes until 1961.

Richard Dimbleby — Commentator and presenter.

Derek Burrell-Davis — Leading OB producer – launched BBC TV in the North, returning to London in 1955. Specialised in circus OBs.

Bill Cotton — Contract LE producer with BBC from 1956. Produced *Six-Five Special*, *Show Band Show*, and his father's *Billy Cotton Band Show*.

Denis Forman — First producer to work on *What The Papers Say*.

Paul Fox — Scriptwriter for Television Newsreel; devised and edited *Sportsview*.

Bimbi Harris — Vision mixer and first woman to operate a TV camera at the BBC.

Joan Kemp-Welch — One of the first woman directors in TV, former theatre director who joined Associated-Rediffusion when it started, and won many major awards for her work.

GERALD
BEADLE
(*BBC*)

SIDNEY
BERNSTEIN
(*Granada*)

HOWARD
THOMAS
(*ABC*)

JOHN McMILLAN (*ARTV*)

VAL PARNELL (*ATV*)

The men at the top 1956

Bernard Wilkie and *Jack Kine* — Visual effects pioneers. Creating the effects for George Orwell's *1984* was one of their biggest challenges during the 50s.

Bill Ward – Producer with BBC Television until 1955, then offered head of LE at ATV on Bob Hope's recommendation.

Sir Kenneth Clark — First chairman of the ITA.

Harry Alan Towers — Ex-Radio Normandie, Managing Director of Towers of London Ltd, one of the first 'indie' production companies; made hundreds of film programmes for ATV.

Howard Thomas — Managing Director of ABC Television, and one of the greatest influences on ITV.

Roy Thomson — Canadian newspaper magnate who was first Chairman of Scottish Television – who once foolishly described having an ITV franchise as akin to 'having a licence to print money'.

Aidan Crawley — ITN's first Editor-in-Chief, who created an entirely new kind of television news. He resigned when the ITV companies tried to trim down the news operations, and joined the BBC.

Robin Day — One of the first ITN newscasters.

Christopher Chataway — Former champion athlete, first ITN newscaster.

Lord Townsend — Chairman of Anglia, brought together the group and moulded one of the most respected of the ITV companies.

Sydney Newman — Head of Drama for ABC.

Key Programmes 1950-59

Andy Pandy (BBC, from 11 Jun 1950) — The first *Watch With Mother* programme. Maria Bird wrote, narrated and designed.

The Quatermass Experiment (BBC, from 18 Jul 1953) — Seat-gripping sci-fi series by Nigel Kneale, produced by Rudolph Cartier.

Panorama (BBC, from 11 Nov 1953) — Current affairs programme, first hosted by Max Robertson, then Richard Dimbleby when it moved to Monday nights.

Dixon of Dock Green (BBC, from 9 Jul 1955) — Police series written by Ted Willis. Jack Warner played PC Dixon. Producer: Douglas Moodie.

The Adventures of Robin Hood (ATV/Sapphire, from 25 Sep 1955) — Starred Richard Greene. First hit ITV film adventure series.

What The Papers Say (Granada, from 1956) — Weekly press review – still running.

Hancock's Half Hour (BBC, from 6 Jul 1956) — Transferred from radio. Tony Hancock and Sid James starred in one of the BBC's most successful sitcoms.

ABC Armchair Theatre (ABC, from 8 Jul 1956) — Sunday night screening of single plays. Producer: Dennis Vance; later Sydney Newman from 1958.

This Week (ARTV, from 1956-93) — Weekly current affairs programme regarded by many as the best of its kind on British TV.

Six-Five Special (BBC, from 16 Feb 1957) — First TV pop show. Comperes were Pete Murray and Jo Douglas who co-produced with Jack Good.

Tonight (BBC, from 18 Feb 1957) — Daily early evening topical magazine with Cliff Michelmore, was the model for all that followed. Producer: Donald Baverstock.

Looking and Seeing (ARTV, 13 May 1957) — First schools TV programme – presented by ARTV announcer Redvers Kyle. Producer: Sydney King.

Emergency Ward 10 (ATV, from 1957) — Hit twice-weekly medical soap created by Tessa Diamond who misunderstood a documentary brief from Bill Ward, and scripted a drama instead. Producer: Antony Kearey.

American Imports — Popular 50s US film series included *I Love Lucy, The Burns & Allen Show, The Phil Silvers Show, Highway Patrol* and *Wells Fargo*.

The Black-and-White Minstrel Show (BBC, from 2 Sep 1957) — An instant hit.

Monitor (BBC, from 2 Feb 1958) — The first successful arts programme, edited and presented by Huw Wheldon.

The Spread of Television 1950-59

1951	BBC	North of England
1952	BBC	Central Scotland
		South Wales & West of England
1953	BBC	North East England
		Belfast
		Brighton
		Isle of Man
1954	BBC	Central Southern England
		Aberdeen
		South West England
1955	BBC	East Anglia
		Northern Ireland
		Channel Islands
	ITA	London and Home Counties
1956	BBC	Cumbria and Borders
	ITA	Midlands
		North of England
1957	BBC	Cardigan Bay coast
		Moray Firth
		Londonderry
	ITA	Central Scotland
1958	BBC	South East England
		Folkstone
		North of Scotland
		Orkney
	ITA	South Wales & West of England
		Central Southern England
1959	BBC	Peterborough
	ITA	North East England
		East Anglia
		Northern Ireland

The First ITV Programme Contractors

London
 Associated-Rediffusion (weekdays)
 Associated TeleVision (weekends)

Midlands
 Associated TeleVision (weekdays)
 ABC Television (weekends)

North
 Granada TV Network (weekdays)
 ABC Television (weekends)

Central Scotland
 Scottish Television (all week)

South Wales & West of England
 TWW (all week)

Central Southern England
 Southern Television (all week)

North East England
 Tyne Tees Television (all week)

East Anglia
 Anglia TV (all week)

Northern Ireland
 Ulster TV (all week)

IV
Never Had It So Good
The 1960s
The decade in which TV grew up

BBC Television might have celebrated its 21st anniversary in 1957 but its enforced war years of suspended animation meant that it didn't really come of age until the 1960s. During this decade the ITV Network reached completion, and for the first time a choice of programmes became almost universally available. Extended programme hours, more channels, more transmitters and an ever-expanding audience, maturing television techniques, the introduction of colour and the challenge of increased competition all contributed to a decade that was rich in exciting and challenging new ideas in television.

The 60s began with yet another Committee of Inquiry (Chairman, Sir Harry Pilkington): to consider the future structure of British TV and the possible allocation of a third channel.

When Pilkington reported in June 1962, the BBC were embarrassed by the effusive and laudatory terms with which it described the Corporation. But if Pilkington painted the BBC as 'whiter than white', it saw the ITV Network and the ITA as in urgent need of overhaul. It was highly critical of much of ITV's output, and came out in favour of a complete reconstruction of the commercial system in which the ITA would sell the advertising, and schedule the programmes, which it would commission from the programme makers. Pilkington was, in essence, opposed to the philosophy of the market-place.

There was an immediate outcry from the ITV companies – "The best place for this report is the waste paper basket," said Peter Cadbury, the flamboyant chairman and joint Managing Director of Westward Television who was reported to have organised a garden party at which Sir Harry was burned in effigy along with copies of his report! And the press were, for once, on ITV's side. Pilkington was seen as having "a haughty conviction that whatever is popular must be bad" (*Daily Telegraph*); "its diagnoses are often good but its main remedy is fantastic" (*Daily Mail*); and it "tells the public to go to

Brand-new STV master control – circa 1960

Hell" (*Daily Mirror*).

The government clearly got more than it bargained for from Pilkington, and smartly swept most of its recommendations under the carpet. Instead it issued two White Papers which, whilst authorising the BBC to start a second channel on UHF in 1964, left the ITA and its charges substantially untouched whilst attacking excessive ITV profits, giving the ITA greater regulatory powers over programming, and refusing ITV a second channel.

The fortunes of the commercial broadcasters were rather mixed in the early part of the decade as the further expansion of ITV met with a variety of obstacles, some political, some financial. As the ITA was persuaded to advertise franchises for increasingly lesser-populated areas, the viability of contractors came into question. This was further complicated by the issue of overlaps with existing contractors.

In the case of Westward, Peter Cadbury made it clear with characteristic directness that, in his view, TWW was a Welsh company which had no business to claim audiences south of the Bristol Channel – a claim which did nothing for intercompany relations. It was also a fact that however much Cadbury huffed and puffed, TWW's signal could clearly be picked up in considerable chunks of the Westward region, and since TWW had come on air first, Westward would have an uphill battle to persuade viewers to change their aerials.

The same situation occurred in Dundee, where at the same time as Grampian Television was coming on air the ITA had increased the power of the

**The Beatles helping presenter *Morag Hood*
with her makeup on STV's *Roundup* 1962**

STV transmitter at Black Hill: thus Grampian had to joust for audiences in the jute city. The Post Office, which had continuing difficulties in providing necessary network and transmitter links on time, exacerbated the situation by initially forcing Grampian to take the same network feed as STV, thereby preventing them from establishing a different identity, except when STV weren't using their network lines.

In both cases, after much debate within the ITA and the companies, the transmitter rentals were reduced in order to prevent serious financial difficulties. Indeed, this was to become a regular formula for the protection of the weaker members of the ITV 'family', who in some cases were also subsidised by the provision of 'cut price' network programmes, and in the case of Westward, an agreement to absorb redundant staff into other ITV companies.

But none of these formulae was able to save the life of the ITV station that perished in its infancy. Wales (West & North) Television – otherwise known as Teledu Cymru – was not merely handicapped by an unwieldy name, forced upon it when TWW objected to the company describing itself simply as 'Wales TV'. The ITA had first considered offering to TWW those transmitters covering the northern and western parts of the principality, but felt obliged, as a result of nationalistic pressure, to offer the contract to a Welsh-based company who would provide some Welsh-language programming in peaktime. The recipient of this contract was a group who made it clear that profits would be secondary to programme expansion.

One of the three transmitters to be provided by the ITA – at Moel-y-Parc, serving Flintshire and Denbigh – had a massive overlap with the service area of the existing Winter Hill transmitter in Lancashire. Granada TV were already providing Welsh language programmes in the afternoons. The Post Office informed the ITA that their Minister would be disinclined to allow the Moel-y-Parc station to be built unless its contractor provided 50% locally originated material, two thirds of which was to be in peak hours. This was an impossible request since even the profitable London-based AR-TV produced just 12.5 hours a week of its own material!

The Post Office demands were eventually negotiated down to a minimum of ten hours a week of Welsh language material, all in good evening viewing hours. But they were still more than a small company could withstand. First, network programme costs to WWN were reduced (which meant that the rest of the network subsidised the company to the tune of some £150,000 a year). Then TWW, and subsequently the network, provided all their programmes free. The enthusiastic but inexperienced officers of the company overstretched their resources, and the ITA conceded in March 1963 that WWN would not have to pay its already deferred transmitter rentals, reducing them instead to a peppercorn £100 a year.

Wales (West & North) ceased all local production, made 80 staff redundant and, in January 1964, had no option but to agree to become a subsidiary of TWW, by which time TWW knew they had been re-appointed as contractor for the combined areas. Thus WWN faded to oblivion. But as WWN departed the scene BBC2 was born.

BBC2 launch symbol, kangaroos _Hullabaloo and Custard_

In the *Radio Times*, Kenneth Adam – the BBC's Director of Television – was at pains to explain to prospective viewers in London and the south east, all the things that the channel would not be. It would not be an invitation to watch more, to seduce viewers away from ITV, to undermine the importance of BBC1, to menace BBC Radio. It was not, he asserted, staffed by an elite, and it was not a new piece of push-button machinery.

On the eve of the launch, after some months of test transmissions, a Service of Dedication from Westminster Abbey was the first actual programme to be screened on the new 625-line service. The programmes scheduled for BBC2's opening night proper, 20 April 1964, included a fireworks display billed as *Off With A Bang*. The network did indeed launch with an almighty bang, as a major fire at Battersea Power Station deprived Television Centre (not to mention much of London!) of its electricity supply for the whole evening, and blacked out the fledgling channel before it even got underway.

Instead, announcements from the unaffected news studios at Alexandra Palace assured viewers, whose TV sets were still working, that BBC2 would launch the next day (as it did with Play School at 11am on 21 April) whilst BBC1 showed a standby movie from Birmingham and thanked its lucky stars that Panorama, that evening, was coming live from Liverpool.

Although little of the decade was free from the rigours of television politics, viewers were only aware of ever-growing programme choice, disrupted sporadically by industrial disputes, a phenomenon new to television.

The catalogue of significant programmes shown during the period would fill a volume on its own. *Coronation Street* made its first appearance in December 1960 with Elsie Lappin handing over her corner shop to new owner Florrie Lindley, Ken Barlow's younger brother mending his bicycle on the living room table, and Elsie Tanner's son newly released from prison.

Outstanding contributions emerged from every possible field of programming. The rich vein of drama owed much of its influence to Canadian, Sydney Newman, who previously headed ABC's drama department, and subsequently the BBC's from 1963. On ABC's *Armchair Theatre* he built a formidable team of producers, like Leonard White who created series like *The Avengers*, *Out Of This World* and other rating successes. He introduced Harold Pinter, Alun Owen, Peter Luke and Angus Wilson to television, and at the BBC presided over dramas as diverse as *Cathy Come Home*, *The Forsyte Saga* and

Dr Who in his first incarnation – played by **William Hartnell**

the Corporation's first twice-weekly soap, *Compact*. Early success on ITV with sci-fi series, like *Pathfinders to Venus*, led to the creation of *Dr Who* under producer Verity Lambert at the BBC. It was Newman who reorganised BBC drama into three departments, separating series and serials from plays, and his loss was deeply felt when he quit television to become a movie producer in 1967.

ATV kept the viewers glued to ITV screens with *Danger Man* (1960), *The Saint* (1962), *Gideon's Way* (1964), *The Baron* (1966), *The Prisoner* (1967), *The Champions* (1968), *Department S* (1969) and *Randall And Hopkirk (Deceased)* (1969) – all popular film drama series which remain at the very top of satellite programme planners' shopping lists today.

Satire was around long before the 60s, but had never been presented to a mass audience until the advent of *That Was The Week That Was*. It launched in November 1962 as a live and dangerous late Saturday night revue with David Frost, Millicent Martin, Kenneth Cope, David Kernan, Roy Kinnear, Bernard Levin, Lance Percival and Willie Rushton. Ned Sherrin produced. *TW3* was aborted after a year: it had not only shocked housewife Mrs Mary Whitehouse into forming a protest group, but offended the BBC's governors sufficiently to warrant the death penalty.

It was also undeniably popular and the BBC's Director-General, Hugh Greene, tactfully attributed its demise to the "difficulties of maintaining its political content in an election year". In fact, it begat *Not So Much A Programme...*, *The Late Show*, *BBC3*, and other satirical series. It also led to

The *Monty Python* crew – their circus began in 1969

phenomenal success for its young presenter – whose award-winning *Frost Report* with John Cleese, Ronnie Barker and Ronnie Corbett led first to his weekly Rediffusion show, and latterly to the thrice-weekly LWT series, *Frost on...* featuring legendary jousts with controversial characters like Dr Emil Savundra.

The arts and sciences were well catered for too, with programmes like ABC's Sunday arts magazine *Tempo*, and the BBC's *Omnibus*, *Horizon* and *Tomorrow's World*. As Man landed on the moon BBC and ITV were there, with James Burke apparently permanently incarcerated in the BBC's 'space studio' and ITV pulling off its longest-ever single show with the 15-hour-long variety and actuality *Man On The Moon* on 20 July 1969.

Sixties' comedy didn't just rely on situations, although many sitcoms like *Sykes*, *Here's Harry*, *The Rag Trade*, *Dad's Army*, *Please Sir!* and *Father Dear Father* pulled in mass audiences. Rediffusion introduced two series which had a lasting effect on television comedy. For children, Daphne Shadwell directed *Do Not Adjust Your Set* which brought together Eric Idle, Terry Jones and Michael Palin as writer-performers together with David Jason, Denise Coffey and the Bonzo Dog Doo Dah Band for an off-the-wall series that won the Prix Jeunesse Gold Medal in 1968. At the same time David Frost was producing *At Last The*

1948 Show for grown-ups with John Cleese, Graham Chapman, Tim Brooke-Taylor, Aimi MacDonald and Marty Feldman.

A year later, on 5 October 1969, Cleese and Chapman joined forces with Idle, Jones and Palin, and cartoonist Terry Gilliam, to create Monty Python's Flying Circus for a not always totally appreciative BBC1.

As the ITV companies built up their fleets of outside broadcast vehicles, and the government continued to exclude outside broadcasts from restrictions on broadcasting hours, more and more sport filled the screens. *World of Sport* – at first fronted by veteran broadcaster Eamonn Andrews, and later by Dickie Davis, the former host of Southern's news magazine *Day by Day* – was ITV's answer to BBC1's long-running Saturday afternoon *Grandstand*.

Not all children of the 60s had it easy. ATV launched its first five-days-a-week strip soap on 2 November 1964, but it took eight years to be fully networked. It was created by the successful writing team of Hazel Adair and Peter Ling, whose previous work had included *Mrs Dale's Diary* for radio and the BBC's *Compact*. Together with producer Reg Watson they formulated *Crossroads*, a tale of Midlanders set loosely in a motel, which allowed a constant succession of new characters to supplement the continuing key roles of motel owner Meg Richardson and her family.

Meg was played by Noele Gordon, a television veteran in the truest sense since she had been employed by John Logie Baird in 1938 to sit in front of experimental colour TV cameras at his Crystal Palace workshop. She joined ATV at its inception, and was the popular presenter of everything from fashion shows to *Lunch Box* and her own series *HI-T With Noele Gordon*.

1968 brought franchise reshuffles. The regulator claimed to be merely fulfilling its duties to the best of its abilities. But to some it seemed that the ITA

Noele Gordon in *Crossroads*

An ITV 'Advertising Magazine'
with host *Drew Russell* in pinstripes

considered itself obliged to make changes in order to prove that it wasn't afraid of flexing its powers, while to others the Authority was merely playing out the more absurd consequences of the Television Act.

As a result, a fifth major ITV contractor was created by removing Yorkshire from the north of England franchise area, and awarding the licence to Yorkshire Television. Not for the first time, the ITA was impressed by applications from star television practitioners, and awarded the weekend London licence to David Frost's star-studded London Weekend consortium. They also chose to deprive TWW of its licence – in spite of no known default on its part that might warrant the death penalty – and gave it instead to Lord Harlech's group, which included the familiar faces of Richard Burton, Stanley Baker, Harry Secombe, Geraint Evans and broadcasters John Morgan, and Wynford Vaughan-Thomas.

TWW's immediate protests were dismissed – they had known, after all, that licence renewal could never be assumed to be automatic – and the company eventually handed over its contract to Harlech three months early, in return for £500,000.

The ITA had already decided that the Midlands and Northwest would now be seven-day licences, and they awarded those to ATV and Granada, respectively. Thus they created for themselves the problem of what to do with ABC Television and Rediffusion, with only the London weekday licence left undecided. The Authority could not bring themselves to eliminate either company from the ITV family, and forced a shotgun marriage.

Rediffusion's chairman, Sir John Spencer Wills, was devastated. His company had done more than any to preserve and protect the ITV system when it was at its weakest, and had an impeccable track record when it came to programme making. Wills did not know that two of his executives – Programme Controller Cyril Bennett and Sales Director Guy Paine, who both appeared before the ITA during the company's

Lady Penelope **from** *Thunderbirds.* **Her 'voice' was** *Sylvia Anderson* **who became a successful US TV executive**

renewal interviews – had also subsequently appeared in identical roles on behalf of the London Weekend group.

With the smell of treachery hanging in the air the unwilling coupling of the two companies was forcibly completed. Thames Television was the result. That ABC Television had taken control of the reins was obvious from the moment Thames went on the air: its opening music ("Perpetuum Mobile") was the same as ABC had used in the Midlands and North.

The franchise changes dislocated some 3,000 television employees, and destabilised labour relations within ITV for some time, with a succession of strikes and disruptions. The ITA even went well beyond its powers to eliminate regionally-produced TV programme journals. With some prompting from the new LWT, ITV was arm-twisted into accepting *TV Times* as a national programme journal. All the companies were shareholders except Channel, who were allowed to go on publishing their *Channel Viewer*.

But development in the 60s went hand-in-hand with dislocation. ABC Television's pioneering tests with the German PAL colour system were to triumph over the BBC's trials using the American NTSC system. BBC2 got the go-ahead to launch colour in 1967 and did so ahead of any other European country when it started what BBC2 Controller David Attenborough coyly referred to as "the launching programmes" on 1 July 1967 with live coverage of Wimbledon, and *A City of Magnificent Intentions*, Anthony Howard's personal documentary about Washington DC.

The 'launching programmes' – which amounted to around five hours a week, at first only on transmitters in the major parts of England – were in advance of the full BBC2 colour service from all transmitters which began on 2 December 1967. ITV and BBC1 were to follow closely behind, with the start of colour on the popular channels in London, the Midlands and the North on 15 November 1969, although the rest of the UK joined in, piecemeal, with colour finally reaching the Channel Islands as late as 1976.

As the decade ended, BBC staff agonised over the implications of the Corporation's policy document 'Broadcasting in the Seventies', and black-and -white seemed to be a thing of the past – except for *Crossroads*' viewers in London who were still many episodes behind as a side-effect of those franchise frolics. Television's adolescent years were now behind: a harsher reality lay ahead.

Significant Dates 1960-69

29 Jun 1960	First programme from BBC Television Centre.
14 Apr 1951	First relay from the USSR.
1 May 1961	Government imposes TV ad duty.
Dec 1961	Equity instructs its members not to work for ITV as result of a pay dispute.
Jun 1962	Pilkington Committee Report.
11 Jul 1962	First Satellite transmissions from USA via Telstar.
31 Jul 1963	Television Act 1963 extends ITA's life until 1976.
5 Oct 1963	BBC TV starts adult education.
8 Jan 1964	ITA announces programme contracts for 3 years from July 1964.

20 Apr 1964	BBC2 opens in London – power failure at Battersea means no programmes.
21 Apr 1964	BBC2 opens properly – first programme is *Play School.*
15 Feb 1965	Two-channel ITV service in South Wales for TWW.
24 May 1965	First UHF test transmissions using PAL colour.
10 Oct 1965	BBC1 shows first Hindi programme for Asian communities.
Jan 1966	Government extends ITV contracts by a year.
2 Jun 1966	Live television pictures shown from moon's surface.
22 Dec 1966	ITA announces changes to ITV 'map'.
11 Jun 1967	ITA announces new contractors for 1968-74; in come Thames HTV, LWT, Yorkshire; out goes TWW.
1 Jul 1967	First regular BBC2 colour transmissions.
3 Jul 1967	*News at Ten* begins on ITV.
30 Jul 1968	New ITV programme companies take over.
19 Sep 1968	*TV Times* becomes national ITV programme journal.
20 Jul 1969	First moon landing shown live on all channels.
8 Sep 1969	ITA begins London UHF colour tests.
15 Nov 1969	Colour begins on BBC1 and Thames/LWT/ATV/Granada/Yorkshire.

Prominent People 1960-69

Hugh Carleton Greene — Director-General of the BBC from 1959-69.

David Attenborough — Controller of BBC2 programmes from 1965, Director of Programmes BBC1 and BBC2 1968-72.

Huw Wheldon — Head of Documentary Programmes 1963-65, Controller of Programmes 1965, Managing Director BBC TV 1968-75.

Gerry Anderson — Creator and director of puppet film series including *Thunderbirds* and *Stingray*.

Gerry Anderson,
creator of many cult
puppet series from
Stingray* to *Thunderbirds

Richard Cawston — Leading BBC documentary maker, who produced *This is the BBC, Television Around the World* and *Royal Family*.

James McTaggart — Respected BBC drama man who produced *Up The Junction*.

Ken Loach — Leading drama director whose work included *Cathy Come Home* and *Up The Junction*.

Tony Warren — Creator of *Coronation Street*.

Howard Steele — Chief Engineer at ABC until 1967, then the ITA's Chief Engineer. Responsible for much development work on colour TV.

Lew Grade — Deputy Managing Director, then Deputy Chairman and MD, then eventually Chairman, ATV.

Charles Hill (Lord Hill of Luton) — Chairman of the ITA 1963-67; Chairman of the BBC 1967-73.

Howard Thomas — Managing Director, first of ABC Television, then Thames.

Sir Robert Fraser — Director-General, ITA 1954-70.

Denis Forman — Joint Managing Director, later Chairman and MD, and eventually Chairman ATV.

Key Programmes 1960-69

Coronation Street (Granada, from 7 Dec 1960) — Britain's longest-running soap.

The Avengers (ABC, from 18 Mar 1961) — Julie Stevens played Venus Smith, then producer Leonard White put Honor Blackman into leather as Cathy Gale, and the rest is history.

Survival (Anglia, from 1961) — Long-running natural history series.

Z Cars (BBC, from 2 Jan 1962) — Gritty northern police drama series.

Steptoe & Son (BBC, from 7 Jun 1962) — Alan Simpson and Ray Galton's evergreen creation with Wilfrid Brambell and Harry H Corbett.

A youthful *Ken Barlow* in *Coronation Street*

Honor Blackman   *by Richard Cole*

That Was The Week That Was (BBC, Nov 1962) — A live and dangerous late Saturday night revue with David Frost, Millicent Martin, Kenneth Cope, David Kernan, Roy Kinnear.

Dr Who (BBC, from 23 Nov 1963) — William Hartnell was the first doctor.

Mogul (BBC1, from 1965) — John Elliott's drama series about the intrigues of the oil industry ran until 1972 – under the name *The Troubleshooters* in the UK from 1966, but as *Mogul* for the rest of the world.

Till Death Us Do Part (BBC1, from 6 Jun 1966) — Johnny Speight created Alf Garnett to be loathed. The public loved him.

Ray Brooks and *Carol White* in *Cathy Come Home*

Cathy Come Home (BBC1, 16 Nov 1966) — Jeremy Sandford's documentary about homelessness.

The Forsyte Saga (BBC2, from 7 Jan 1967) — Donald Wilson's definitive dramatisation of Galsworthy's story of a prosperous English family.

Nationwide (BBC1, from 9 Sep 1969) — Michael Barratt linked this nightly live round-Britain evening news programme.

Monty Python's Flying Circus (BBC2, from Oct 1969-1974) — Off-beat and often tasteless comedy sketch show written and performed by an ex-Cambridge group became one of the most influential programmes on a generation of viewers. Producer: Ian Macnaughton.

The ITV Programme Contractors

SW England	Westward Television	
The Borders	Border Television	
NE Scotland	Grampian Television	
Channel Islands	Channel Television	
West & North Wales	Teledu Cymru (Wales [West & North] Television)	
From July 1968		
Wales & West of England	Harlech Television	
Yorkshire	Yorkshire Television	
London	Thames Television	(weekdays)
	London Weekend Television	(weekends)
Midlands	ATV Network	(all week)
NW England	Granada TV Network	(all week)

V
Colouring In, Blacking Out
The 70s

A rocky
yet creative decade

There are no golden ages, and for Britain the 1970s – with their industrial confrontations, political instability, sometimes rampant inflation, and violence on the streets of Northern Ireland – were far from perfect. All these tendencies had direct impact on the television industry, as much as anything. In January 1974 the energy crisis provoked the government into closing television down at 10.30pm; nine months later, the impact of that on the national life became evident.

Yet it was also, for television, a decade of colour, of high ambition often backed by big money, of creative talents coming to maturity and of the regulatory screw being loosened a little. We were actually allowed TV in the afternoon, if anyone could afford to give it us.

No decade, of course, would be complete without at least one government Committee of Inquiry. The Annan Committee, under Lord Annan, was given its brief in May 1970 by Harold Wilson's government, but it was stood down a month later after the Conservatives' election victory. Labour returned to power in 1974, and Annan was again given the green light. It took almost three years to consider its recommendations.

As with all such committees, many of the Annan proposals fell upon stony ground, although in some cases it was eventually to prove surprisingly fertile. Within its 522 pages and 174 recommendations it proposed the establishment of a fourth channel, to be run by yet another new body – the Open Broadcasting Authority. It would accept programmes from a number of sources, including the ITV companies, the Open University and, most significantly, independent producers who would also be given greater access to BBC and ITV.

Whilst its proposal to set up two new Authorities were not subsequently adopted by the government, others – including the setting-up of a joint audience

Transmission controllers at STV – 1974

measurement system by the broadcasters, the establishment of the Broadcasting Complaints Committee, the ending of the listings monopoly and, of course, the model for Channel Four – would come to fruition in the 80s.

Although no new TV channels were to launch during the decade, it did see the start of the much-vaunted Open University in 1971, which quietly established itself as one of the most important innovations in tertiary education this century, its academic centre working with integral television and radio support from the BBC.

More technical advances were initially of little interest to the average viewer, although they offered a hint of greater things to come. In April 1973, IBA engineers unveiled their ORACLE system of teletext. Development of the system was rapid, and the BBC launched their CEEFAX service in September 1974, followed by a regular ORACLE service on ITV ten months later. Few teletext sets were available and the converters were expensive, so the audience for the new service was slow to build.

In May 1978 the European Space Agency launched an orbital test satellite to conduct some experiments into direct satellite broadcasting in the

12GHz band. Little notice was taken of it at the time, and it was not until the next decade that serious use was made of the satellite.

And there was one significant false start. In mid-decade, at an RTS Cambridge Convention, Philips demonstrated their new videocassette recorder and videodisc – predicting that the former would become a professional tool, the latter the domestic device. By the end of the 70s, the fight for the home market was on, but for the VCR and between BetaMax and VHS.

Although the 1970s began with the opening of the last 405-line VHF transmitter at Newhaven in Sussex on 3 August 1970, the thrust of both BBC and ITA engineers was directed towards the 625-line UHF colour services. There was a rapid increase in the commissioning of UHF transmitters. At the start of 1970 there were seven transmitters and no relays radiating three-channel colour programmes; by the end of 1978 these totals were 51 and 384 respectively.

And where the transmissions went, the receivers followed. The public took to colour TV with enthusiasm. At 31 March 1970, there were 273,397 colour licences in force, and 15.6 million mono. The following year, the radio and radio/TV licences were abolished. At 31 March 1980, colour licences stood at 12.13 million (mono, 6.25).

At the same time, the level of the colour fee rose from £11 at the start of the decade to £34 at the end of 1979. Despite inflation there were real gains here. ITV, able to sell its airtime at new premium prices as colour spread, saw similar gains.

Many of the apparently insurmountable problems of programme distribution had also been overcome. A steerable multi-antennae system which the IBA's acronym-partial engineers had christened SABRE brought clear colour pictures to the Channel Islands – the last of the ITV regions to begin colour transmissions (on 26 July 1976).

Four days later a chain of link stations constructed across the Highlands was brought into service, allowing the main station on Stornoway to begin transmissions. These were interrupted for some months when a remote and inaccessible massive passive deflector at Sgurr Marcasaidh was blown over in a gale, requiring major efforts and a helicopter to restore. It was the occasion of one of the two most spectacular service interruptions in the history of British television.

The other was at Emley Moor in Yorkshire. In March 1969, severe ice caused the collapse of the 1,256ft tubular steel transmitting mast, and it not only blacked out Yorkshire Television completely for several days, but dealt a serious blow to plans for UHF transmissions to the area. But thanks to superhuman efforts and a couple of hastily procured and erected standby masts, BBC1 and ITV UHF transmissions began on time. By the beginning of 1971 the IBA had completed construction of the replacement slim 14,000-ton concrete tower, which stands some 1,100 feet high.

The problems associated with bringing colour pictures to the Shetland Isles were solved when an unmanned diesel-powered microwave link station came into operation on the bird sanctuary island of Fair Isle, on Christmas Eve 1976.

Christmas 1970 had been a frustrating one for the proud new owners of early, massive (in price and dimensions) dual-standard colour sets. A dispute with ITV engineers over extra pay for handling colour signals meant a return to monochrome pictures on the commercial channel until the middle of February 1971. As a result of many other industrial skirmishes, viewers became

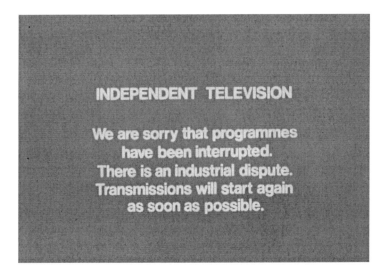

INDEPENDENT TELEVISION

We are sorry that programmes
have been interrupted.
There is an industrial dispute.
Transmissions will start again
as soon as possible.

accustomed through the decade to seeing an apology on their screens for lengthy periods – and not only on the commercial channel.

The removal in 1972 of government restrictions on broadcasting hours led to a gradual increase in programme hours, although the BBC's initial enthusiasm for daytime television in the autumn of 1974 was quickly tempered by a shortage of funds, despite its enhanced revenue the BBC was running a £19 million deficit by the end of 1975, and the little girl on the test card – one Carol

Hersee whose father chaired the committee which designed the card – resumed her afternoon game of noughts and crosses on BBC1 for the remainder of the decade.

When BBC2 scheduled a 5.30pm start to programmes in late 1978, there was union resistance which initially caused teatime programming to be blacked out, and eventually led to a virtual shutdown of both BBC channels just before Christmas.

But by far the worst dispute began in the summer of 1979, when an increasing number of sporadic conflicts within local ITV regions escalated into a total walkout of both technicians and journalists on the afternoon of August 10. While protracted negotiations went on, viewers had to be content with the standard IBA dispute apology caption and tapes of classical music dutifully played out each day from the Authority's temporary national control centre at St Hilary, near Cardiff. It was rumoured at the time that the caption and music were getting a pretty good audience rating (borne out by the subsequent success of Classic FM). The dispute lasted for 11 weeks, and it was not until 5.45pm on 24 October that viewers were greeted by the Mike Sammes singers bidding them

'Welcome Home to ITV'.

The decade was a stable one in terms of ITV franchises, but technology had various effects on local programming. The introduction of new, lightweight cameras and camcorders (dubbed ENG – Electronic News Gathering – because at first it was not deemed of sufficient high quality for entertainment programming) meant that for the first time it became possible to divide ITV regions and provide different local news programmes to different transmitters. ITV companies began modest experiments in this field.

Although it eschewed the notion of Pay-TV on cable (a "ravenous parasite," according to Annan) the government recognised the unique ability of the medium to provide truly local services. Five experimental local channels were licensed for operation on existing relay systems. The first of these, in Greenwich, was launched in July 1972. Most made use of 'portable' camcorders which were, in fact, only just light enough to be carried by one person and resembled a large fully-loaded rucksack!

The schedules consisted mainly of local news, interviews and discussions, often in black-and-white, produced and presented by volunteers. All eventually closed through lack of funding since the relay operators – obliged to bear the cost of the experiments without the benefit of subscription revenues – realised their altruism was not about to win them the ultimate prize. But they helped focus the idea of viewer access (one of the principles espoused by the more radical mainstream broadcasters in the 70s) and paved the way for more ambitious experiments in the next decade. In the case of the man chosen to run the experiment in Swindon – Richard Dunn – it led to a distinguished and high-level career in broadcast television, until his premature death in August 1998.

Viewer access at a different level lay behind the row over ITV's Belmont, Lincs, transmitter. In July 1974 Belmont was handed over to Yorkshire Television – with the proviso that it would continue to put out local news programmes for the East of England. So Anglia made a special bulletin, then passed it to Yorkshire for transmission from Belmont!

Increasing technical sophistication was not the only influence on programming during the decade. There was more money available to spend on programmes than ever before and, since it was concentrated on just three channels, much of it was evident on the screen.

But increased ease of communication was certainly behind such advances as the coverage of the 1970 General Election, which saw the BBC's TV and radio journalists combining for their biggest ever exercise, and launched the BBC/ITN competition at a new level. Similarly, not just colour, but technological progress gave the decade's coverage of world sporting events a new dimension.

The success of Lord Clark's pioneering *Civilisation* on BBC2 spawned a line of global 'coffee-table' documentary series, with Alistair Cooke's *America* and Jacob Bronowski's *The Ascent Of Man* (1974) as a pinnacle. Thames's *The World At War* (1973) established a lasting benchmark for living-history documentary. In *Life On Earth* (1979) David Attenborough and the BBC Natural History Unit did the same for wildlife.

Yet, at the same time, the smaller-scale or more specialist techniques were probing boundaries, aided by lighter cameras and faster stock, as in Paul Watson's real-life saga *The Family,* and Roger Graefs *The Space Between Words* – and current affairs series from *World In Action* and *This Week* to *Nationwide* and *Panorama* sought new freedoms.

Sumptuous costume dramas abounded. In 1970, BBC1 offered *The Six Wives of Henry VIII* with Keith Michell as the King, and a year later *Elizabeth R* with Glenda Jackson as the Queen. *Poldark*, based on the romantic novels by Winston Graham, was an instant hit in 1975.

Tolstoy's epic *War & Peace* was two years in the making, and when it was shown

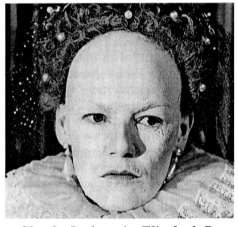

Glenda Jackson in *Elizabeth R*

on BBC2 in 1972 an 84-page *Radio Times War & Peace* special, all in colour, offered viewers help to sort out what the 20 episodes were all about, as well as providing convenient pin-ups of Anthony Hopkins and Morag Hood. BBC2 also provided *I Claudius* four years later, with Derek Jacobi.

ITV's prolific offerings in this field included Thames's *Jennie – Lady Randolph Churchill* (1974) with Lee Remick taking centre stage in Julian

Mitchell's stories about Winston's mum; and *Edward and Mrs Simpson* (1978), Simon Raven's seven-part series reconstructing the royal romance, with Edward Fox every inch the part. From ATV came *Edward the Seventh* (1975) with Timothy West in the regal role; and *Clayhanger* (1976), Douglas Livingstone's 26-part adaptation of Arnold Bennett's 19th century Staffordshire potteries trilogy.

***Upstairs Downstairs* – Hudson, Ruby and Mrs Bridges discuss life below stairs in LWT's hit drama**

October 1971 saw the debut of *Upstairs, Downstairs*, LWT's long-running series about the lives of a wealthy London family and their servants from 1903. Jean Marsh devised the series with Eileen Atkins, and starred in it alongside Pauline Collins and Gordon Jackson, and it became perhaps a surrogate for a soap in a decade when soaps were drifting out of fashion.

1930s Edinburgh was the setting for *The Prime of Miss Jean Brodie* (STV, 1978), Jay Presson Allen's six-part adaptation of Muriel Spark's tales of a radical school teacher, which starred Geraldine McEwan as Brodie.

From HTV and Germany's TeleMunchen came the television version of Robert Louis Stevenson's quintessentially Scottish tale, *Kidnapped*, with Scots

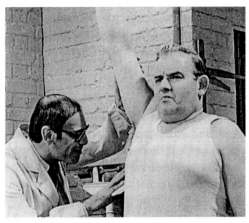

Porridge

actors David McCallum and Bill Simpson. The curious presence of German actor Ekkehardt Beile as David Balfour, however, was a good example of the inevitable artistic compromises prevalent in co-productions of the period.

Jesus of Nazareth (ATV/RAI, 1977) was Franco Zeffirelli's epic New Testament series with Robert Powell as Jesus, Olivia Hussey as Mary (and Claudia Cardinale, so eager to appear, she gladly settled for three lines of dialogue). For ATV's Lew Grade (who set it up) the series was, perhaps, an unexpected addition to his many impressive acheivements.

And yet, again, there was original drama in what now seems abundance. To choose just a few from 1975-7 alone: the politically radical *Leeds United!* and *Days Of Hope* (BBC); the sexually ground-breaking *Naked Civil Servant;* the socially satirical *Rock Follies* (Thames).

And it was the decade in which Dennis Potter wrote *Where Adam Stood* and *Blue Remembered Hills*, had *Brimstone And Treacle* banned in a memorable censorship row, and then (having entered the decade with the less than memorable *Casanova*) arguably signalled the arrival of a new genre with the triumphant mini-series *Pennies From Heaven*.

Many of the classic comedies now playing as seemingly endless re-runs on both

Up Pompeii

terrestrial and satellite channels originated during this decade. *Up Pompeii* (BBC1, 1970) was created by *Carry On* writer, Talbot Rothwell, as a vehicle for Frankie Howerd; *The Lovers* (Granada, 1970) was the first series to feature the talented Richard Beckinsale, who (before his untimely death at the end of the decade) also turned up in *Rising Damp* (YTV, 1974) with Leonard Rossiter, and *Porridge* (BBC1, 1974) with Ronnie Barker.

The late Leonard Rossiter himself was very much a giant of television comedy in the 70s, both as Eric Chappell's wonderfully seedy landlord, Rigsby, and as the born-again average chap Reggie Perrin in David Nobbs' eccentric *Fall and Rise of Reginald Perrin* (BBC1, 1976).

Other comedy classics of the period included: *The Two Ronnies* (Barker and Corbett) set free from assorted David Frost series in 1971; *Last of the Summer Wine* (BBC1, 1973); *Are You Being Served?* (BBC1, 1973); *It Ain't Half Hot Mum* (BBC1, 1974); *The Good Life* (BBC1, 1975); *Fawlty Towers* (BBC2, 1975); *Not the Nine O'Clock News* (BBC2, 1979) –

The Two Ronnies

testament to the strength of Bill Cotton's BBC lighter entertainment group. From ITV came *The Muppet Show* (ATV, 1976); *Bless This House*, Sid James' final series; *Love Thy Neighbour* (Thames, 1972) – the first UK comedy with black stars in Nina Baden-Semper and Rudolph Walker; and *Shelley* (Thames, 1979). Riches indeed.

A golden age? For quite a few of those who lived through them, the 70s were a period of money problems and strife. At that level the groundwork was laid for Mrs Thatcher's onslaught.

At another, it was a time when advancing technology came together with creative confidence, in both commercial and public sectors, to set new standards.

Thames Television's *Love Thy Neighbour*
the first UK comedy with black stars

Significant Dates 1970-79

2 Jul 1970	State Opening of Parliament shown in colour.
3 Aug 1970	ITA VHF station at Newhaven is the last 405-line transmitter to come into service.
29 Aug 1970	BBC suspends Delhi operation when Indian government threatens Corporation for showing film series about India made by Louis Malle for French Television.
Dec 1970	Pay dispute causes ITV programmes to be screened in black-and-white until mid Feb 1971.
3 Jan 1971	The Open University transmits its first programmes.
16 Jun 1971	Lord Reith dies.
3 Oct 1971	BBC Programme Complaints Commission established.
10 Nov 1971	BBC Pebble Mill studios opened by Princess Anne.
19 Jan 1972	Post Office control of broadcasting hours ends.
3 Jul 1972	Experimental local cable TV channel begins at Greenwich.
12 Jul 1972	ITA becomes the Independent Broadcasting Authority.
1 Nov 1972	BBC begins celebrations for its 50th anniversary.
Apr 1973	IBA engineers unveil ORACLE teletext system.
Jan 1974	National power crisis forces TV to close down at 10.30pm every night.
28 Mar 1977	Experimental breakfast-time programmes on YTV & Tyne Tees.

31 May 1977	IBA demonstrates first digital TV studio.
13 Nov 1978	Extension of programme hours on BBC2 is met with union resistance, initially causing teatime programming to be lost, and eventually leading to a blackout of BBC1 and BBC2 just before Christmas.
21 Mar 1979	BBC working party reports on violence on TV – new guidelines established.
10 Aug 1979	Strike by technicians and journalists takes ITV (except for Channel) off the air until Oct 24.
2 Sep 1979	First CEEFAX subtitled programme shown on BBC TV.

Prominent People 1970–79

Sir Charles Curran — BBC's admired Director-General 1969-77, until edged out by conservative Chairman Lord Hill.

Ian Trethowan — BBC Managing Director, Television, then Director-General 1977-82.

Verity Lambert — Noted drama producer, work included *Dr Who* (BBC) and *Budgie* (LWT), before becoming an adventurous Controller of Drama at Thames in 1974.

John Freeman — From left-wing journalist and *Face To Face* interviewer to ambassador to India and the US in the 60s, he became Chairman and Chief Executive Officer of the team who took LWT from near-ruin to a leading role in ITV.

David Nicholas — ITN Editor and Chief Executive.

Brian Tesler — Director of Programmes at Thames until 1974, moved to LWT as First Deputy and then Chief Executive.

Jeremy Isaacs — Took over from Tesler at Thames in 1974, having built major documentary department.

Gus Macdonald — editor of *World In Action* at its most vigorous, then Executive in Charge of Granada's current affairs (features).

Denis Forman — Joint Managing Director at Granada who succeeded Cecil Bernstein as Chairman.

David Plowright — Granada's Programme Controller, who brought his brother-in-law (Laurence Olivier) to ITV.

Cyril Bennett — LWT's charismatic and professional Controller of Programmes from 1971 until his sudden death in 1976, and in whose name one of the RTS's major awards is endowed.

Paul Fox — Started the decade as Controller, BBC1, then made the leap to become YTV's Programme Controller in 1973 and MD in 1976.

Michael Grade — Newcomer to TV in 1973, LWT's energetic Deputy Controller of Programmes (entertainment) rose to Director of Programmes for the latter half of the decade.

John Birt — Current Affairs Producer, first for Granada, then LWT where he created *Weekend World* with Peter Jay. Thence upwards to Controller, Features and Current Affairs.

James MacTaggart — Inspirational drama director who picked up the challenge of the new CSO/chroma-key technology and put it to work in productions like a witty version of *Candide.*

Sir Brian Young — ITA/IBA's Director-General for the whole of the decade

David Attenborough — BBC Television's Director of Programmes, who walked away from his desk (and perhaps the Director-Generalship) to return triumphantly to programme-making.

Bryan Cowgill — BBC TV Head of Sport and OBs, then Controller, BBC1 – and followed Fox to ITV, as Managing Director of Thames as the decade ended.

Aubrey Singer — Head of Features at BBC-TV, then Controller, BBC2.

Key Programmes 1970-79

Aquarius (LWT, from April 1970) — Influential fortnightly arts magazine hosted by editor Humphrey Burton.

Yesterday's Men (BBC1, 17 June 1971) — Controversial *24 Hours* documentary which presented the defeated Labour government in a less than positive light and not surprisingly caused a furore. Presenter: David Dimbleby. Producer: Angela Pope.

The Comedians (Granada, from July 1971) — John Hemp created and produced this simple series which featured comparatively unknown stand-up comedians, almost all of whom subsequently became household names, like Bernard Manning and Tom O'Connor.

The Persuaders (ATV, from 8 Oct 1971) — Lew Grade was the real persuader: he got Tony Curtis and Roger Moore to co-star in this glamour-filled action and adventure film series about an English Lord and his American friend. Terry Nation was story consultant. Robert S. Baker produced.

The Question of Ulster (BBC1, 5 Jan 1972) — Three-hour live debate on the crisis in Northern Ireland, which went ahead despite several attempts to stop the BBC from making it. Ludovic Kennedy chaired.

Newsround (BBC1, from 4 Apr 1972) — John Craven was presenter of this twice-weekly five-minute news bulletin specially compiled for a younger audience, and screened during children's television.

Weekend World (LWT, from Sep 1972) — This live current affairs series started life as a 90-minute programme at 11am on Sunday. Peter Jay was the first presenter. John Birt was the Executive Producer.

The Generation Game (BBC1) — With Bruce Forsyth at the helm it drew huge audiences to kick-start an often all-conquering BBC1 Saturday night schedule and begat two decades of participation shows.

The World At War (Thames, from Sep 1973) — Documentary series about World War II. Produced by Jeremy Isaacs. Narrated by Laurence Olivier.

Rising Damp (Yorkshire, from Dec 1974) — Eric Chappell's classic comedy starring Leonard Rossiter as Rigsby, landlord of some seedy flats inhabited by Richard Beckinsale, Frances de la Tour and Don Warrington. Ronnie Baxter produced and directed.

Muppets: *Kermit* (opposite) and *Miss Piggy*

Fawlty Towers

Fawlty Towers (BBC2, from 19 Sep 1975) — John Cleese and his then wife, Connie Booth, wrote and co-starred with Prunella Scales and Andrew Sachs in this classic farce based on a nightmarish south coast hotel. John Howard Davies was the producer.

The Sweeney (Thames, from Oct 1975) — John Thaw and Dennis Waterman starred in this frequently violent action cop series, produced by Ted Childs, that made the most of lighter cameras.

The Muppet Show (ATV/Henson Associates [Jim Henson, Jon Stone], from 1976) — Proof that puppets and television will always go together as Jim Henson made an international superstar out of the sleeve of his old raincoat!

VI
Dawn of a New Era
The 80s

A turbulent decade
which changed the face of television in this country

From the very start of the decade, change was in the air. And that's how it was to stay, as politics, technologies, people and programming went into continuous flux.

A mere 24 days into the new decade, the IBA announced the creation of a national breakfast-time franchise and invited applications for all of its existing franchises from 1982. A few months later the Home Secretary announced the phased closure of the 405-line VHF transmitter network. The IBA announced the appointment of the Rt. Hon. Edmund Dell as Chairman, and Sir Richard Attenborough as Deputy Chairman of a panel of consultants who, following the enactment of the 1980 Broadcasting Bill, became the first members of the Board of Channel Four Television due to launch at the end of 1982. In November the Home Secretary announced a two-year pay-TV cable experiment in 12 areas of England and Wales.

The first major shock to the television ecology was the announcement of the new ITV franchises made – on 28 December 1980 – in an attempt to minimise any effect on share prices. Forty-three groups had offered to provide ITV services, of which eight were for the new breakfast-time service. The decision not to renew Southern Television's contract shocked some, the enlarged South and Southeast region being awarded instead to Television South, under the direction of James Gatward. Westward Television, chaired by the controversial Sir Peter Cadbury, was replaced by Television South West, with the little-known Kevin Goldstein-Jackson as joint MD (with Peter Battle) and Programme Controller.

The re-awarding of franchises in the new dual region of East and West Midlands, together with the franchises in Northeast England and Yorkshire, also had a dramatic effect. ATV, the longest surviving ITV contractor, was told that it had to be based in the Midlands and make substantial alterations to its shareholdings – with the Lew Grade empire's parent company (Associated Communications Corporation Ltd) allowed only 51% of the capital. The IBA requested a change of name to reflect the creation of a substantially new company: Central Independent Television was the phoenix.

Tyne Tees Television and Yorkshire Television were allowed to retain their franchises provided they ceased to be under the control of Trident

Anna Ford

Television, whose holding in TTT was limited to 20% and YTV to 15% – an ironic condition in the light of the subsequent re-merger in the 90s. All of these changes took place on 1 January 1982 and, as on previous occasions, the IBA declined to give reasons for their decisions, leading, at the end of the decade to a requirement for more accountability. Cold comfort to this round's losers!

But the franchise attracting most attention was the new national breakfast station, due to begin in early 1983. Of the eight applicants, the IBA was most impressed if not seduced by the glamour of TV-am, fronted by David Frost, Anna Ford, Michael Parkinson, Angela Rippon and Robert Kee – dubbed 'The Famous Five'.

The Broadcasting Complaints Commission began its work in the summer of 1981, and around the same time the first joint BBC/ITV audience research – conducted by BARB – was established. The BBC's Royal Charter was renewed until 31 December 31.

In the autumn of that year, Rediffusion launched their Starview Channel in five English towns. It was the first of what the government of the day viewed as 'Pay-TV', although today it would more properly be described as a premium cable TV channel, since viewers were charged a subscription for the service as a whole, rather than for individual movies.

A month later Brian Haynes, producer of a Thames *TV Eye* documentary about US satellite broadcasting in 1979, launched his own television channel. Aimed at cable systems on the European continent, it was the first cable channel to distribute its service via communications satellite, and began full programming service on 26 April 1982, in Norway, Finland, Switzerland and Malta. A year later Haynes' investors were bought out by News International, who changed the name of the service to Sky Channel. It was to be ten years before the full significance of Rupert Murdoch's acquisition was understood.

Meanwhile, more Pay-TV movie services were launched – including the Visionhire experiment in London, which was compiled and played out under contract by the BBC from a continuity suite in Television Centre.

In March 1982 the government announced that it intended to allow the BBC to start broadcasting two television channels by satellite for direct home reception. These DBS (Direct Broadcasting by Satellite – also known as DTH, Direct-To-Home) services were to start in 1986. The long battle of high- versus medium-power satellites was joined.

A few weeks later a group of European Broadcasting Union members ran the first trial pan-European public service satellite experiment. The experimental channel – named Eurikon – was programmed and broadcast by five countries in turn for individual weeks. The IBA were quick to offer their services as co-ordinators of the first week's programmes, starting on 24 May 1982, complete with such gems as: *It's A Knockout* from Italy; a James Joyce documentary from RTE in Ireland; a Pentecostal mass from Brussels Cathedral; and *The Queen Visits Coronation Street* from Granada. The purpose of the venture was to identify the problems associated with this new kind of television, although the reality was a serious case of incest – broadcasters broadcasting to broadcasters with no need to worry about the viewers!

What British viewers could see by now were the test transmissions for the new fourth channel, the final version largely the work of Lord Whitelaw (Margaret Thatcher's Home Secretary) who rejected the plans of Labour's ideologues and his own party's marketeers to create a bold addition to British

 television. Channel Four – a company of which the IBA was the sole shareholder – was to be the first broadcaster-publisher. It would commission programmes from both ITV and independent producers (of whom there were few in 1982) and its 'remit' was to provide a service which was complementary to ITV, innovative, catering for newer audiences and extending the range of programmes available.

Jeremy Isaacs was appointed Chief Executive of Channel Four in January 1981, with Justin Dukes as his deputy and Paul Bonner as Channel Controller, acting as Isaacs' deputy on programme matters. Ellis Griffiths was appointed Chief Engineer.

The service in Wales was to be provided by the Welsh Fourth Channel (S4C) with peak time devoted to programming in the Welsh language. S4C went on air first – at 6pm on 1 November 1982 – with *Croeso i S4C*, a bilingual programme presented by Owen Edwards (S4C's Director). Welsh viewers were to see most of the C4 schedule, but during off-peak hours.

Channel Four itself launched the next day just before 4.45pm with a breathtaking montage of clips from some of its new programmes, followed by

**Countdown, Channel Four's first programme,
with *Richard Whitely* and *Carol Vordeman***

the instantly popular and enduring word game *Countdown*, presented by Richard Whitely, with Ted Moult as scorer. Its first commercial break, however, was less popular. A dispute between the advertising agencies and actors' union over payments to performers for the transmission of commercials on Channel Four meant that in most parts of the country there were no commercials at all, just a caption during breaks, accompanied by the Channel Four theme 'Four Score', which doubtless generated useful royalties for its composer, David Dundas.

For C4 this was more a presentational irritant than a bottom-line blow, since the complex structure of the system meant that the regional ITV companies paid guaranteed predetermined sums to Channel Four in return for the right to sell and transmit the advertising in its breaks.

The character of the new services was neatly summed up in the opening night schedules, even though Isaacs had to construct it from the programmes that happened to be ready.

It included: *The Body Show*, a keep fit series; *People's Court*; the first *Channel Four News* from ITN with Peter Sissons; episode one of *Brookside*; the first Film On Four, *Walter*, from Central TV, starring Ian McKellen; plus *The Comic Strip*.

The hour-long news at 7pm; the soap on a supposedly 'cultural' channel; the gritty social-issue *Film On Four*; the raucous 'alternative' comedy – each drew controversy. The popular press scorned C4 from the word go and viewers were rather slow to warm to it (coverage started at around 80 per cent), but many sampled its wares and both audiences and reputation grew slowly but steadily.

Exactly a month after Channel Four's launch, the government – acting on recommendations of the Hunt Report – gave the green light to the development of broadband cable television systems in the UK, and the creation of new programme channels to serve them. The White Paper was published the following April, the Bill published on 1 December and enacted on 26 June 1984.

The first shoots of the cable industry became visible on 13 January 1984, when Swindon Cable – a long-established relay system owned by Thorn EMI – was licensed to the Home Office to carry a new programme service, Sky Channel. Three days later pop singer Kate Bush symbolically cut the tape to launch the newly rechristened service in the UK. After a number of false starts, in which Government

Crossroads' **Benny Hawkins played by** *Paul Henry* **[1984]**

policy played a key role, the programming side of the British cable industry had at last begun.

Of the three British-owned services which followed Sky on to cable on 29 March 1984 – Music Box, Screensport and The Entertainment Network – none survives today.

The Cable Authority was formally constituted in December 1984, but it was the Home Office that awarded the first 11 pilot cable franchises on 29 November 1983, one of which was the existing Swindon Cable, the first to launch as a broadband system on 17 September 1984.

The majority of the British public were unaware of this new underground movement, and for them the most interesting development was the launch on 17 January 1983 of the BBC's *Breakfast-Time* programme, deliberately pre-empting ITV's new *TV-am* which was to launch on February 1 to mixed fortunes. Early worthy attempts to educate viewers at that hour of the morning were short-lived, and the familiar 'presenters on the couch' format was quickly developed. Within months the founding faces were out of studio and (Frost apart) from boardroom – to be replaced by a new populist regime that launched the glove puppet Roland Rat and the young and streetwise Greg Dyke into the annals.

Meanwhile, the BBC had finally realised the DBS option was a poisoned chalice and, after much consultation with the government, determined to have what it saw as a technological world leader: it was announced in May 1984 that there would be a joint BBC/IBA/ITV DBS consortium instead of a BBC-only one.

In July 1985 the consortium was wound up. The government next asked the IBA to offer the British DBS frequencies to private enterprise through the TV franchise route and, on 11 December 1986, they went to a consortium called British Satellite Broadcasting. They proposed four services on three channels:

Roger Moore – star of *The Saint, The Persuaders* and several
Bond movies – is interviewed by *Paul Hollingdale* for Sky TV

Galaxy (general entertainment); Now (topical programmes); Zig Zag
(children's); and Screen (movies). The IBA said services – for which they would
provide transmission facilities – would start in 'late 1989'. Subsequently two
more channels were awarded to BSB, but they didn't appear until the start of the
new decade. And not for long.

By now the Cable Authority was up and running. More and more new
channels launched themselves, but the tiny cable universe was to grow painfully
slowly as risk and recession hit infrastructure investment.

Out in the mainstream, controversy abounded. In 1980 Antony Thomas's
Death Of A Princess (ATV) caused diplomatic ructions with Saudi Arabia. The
ban on broadcasting the voices of Northern Ireland's illegal organisation hit all
broadcasters.

But the BBC was to take the brunt. *The Observer* newspaper rightly
accused the corporation of allowing MI5 to vet its staff; police seized tapes of a
documentary in the BBC Scotland *Secret Society* series from Broadcasting
House in Glasgow. And a number of high-profile libel cases added to the
tensions that had built up between the Director-General, Alasdair Milne, a fiery

Breakfast Time gave the country the chance to wake up with Frank Bough and his team

programme-maker, and the new Chairman of the Governors, Marmaduke Hussey.

Early in 1987 Milne was called aside from a governor's meeting and summarily dismissed. He was replaced by his deputy, Michael Checkland, a respected manager, who was urged to appoint as his deputy a senior ITV figure, John Birt. The move to reform the management and financing of the BBC was under way. And Checkland would be another victim.

The pressure came from the Thatcher government, symbolised by the setting up of a committee – chaired by a free-market economist, Sir Alan Peacock – on the financing of the BBC. Paradoxically, its report, in July 1986, left the BBC largely unscathed – instead, it loosed the notion of auctioning the commercial airwaves which, as a new Broadcasting Bill and franchise round approached, precipitated the most radical restructuring, job-shedding, union-busting, cost-slashing changes in ITV.

The final twist in this turbulent decade was rich in irony. The Thatcher team's own vision of a world-lead in DBS was dished by one of her own. With BSB still planning, Rupert Murdoch – ace entrepreneur – leapt aboard the new Luxembourg-based Astra satellite and, on 6 February 1989, launched four DBS channels at Britain. Without so much as a by-your-leave.

Other Dates which Made the Decade
~ How the 80s were Shaped ~

1 Dec 1980   BBC Scotland experimentally simulcasts its breakfast-time radio show *Good Morning Scotland* on BBC1 for a week.

12 Oct 1982   Hunt Report is published, recommending the establishment of broadband cable systems.

15 Jul 1983   EBU recommends adoption of C-MAC as standard for DBS.

16 Jan 1984   BBC Elstree Centre opens.

17 Jan 1984   Lightning strikes transmitter mast at Durris, Kincardineshire, blacking out all 4 channels in the Grampian area. Temporary low-power services restored from Redmoss a week later.

29 Mar 1984   Launch of three new cable channels – Music Box, Screensport and TEN – on 22 upgraded relay systems.

1 Sep 1984   Launch of The Children's Channel and Premiere.

May 1985   Peacock Committee, chaired by Sir Alan Peacock, set up to investigate ways of financing the BBC.

2 Jun 1985   TEN – The Entertainment Network – closes. Mirrorvision is launched.

1 Apr 1986   Mirrorvision merges with Premiere.

Jul 1986   Peacock Committee reports, and to the government's dismay it rejects supplementing the advertising fee by accepting advertising.

27 Oct 1986   BBC launches daytime television programming.

30 Jan 1987   Launch of Superchannel.

1 Aug 1987   Launch of MTV Europe.

6 Aug 1987   BBC and ITV agree to government proposals (resulting from the Peacock report) for 25% of their programmes to be produced by independents.

16 May 1988   Home Secretary announces appointment of Broadcasting Standards Council, which meets under chairman Lord Rees-Mogg four months later.

3 Oct 1988   ITV now broadcasting 24 hours a day in all areas.

1 Nov 1988   British Film Institute's *One Day In The Life Of Television* diary exercise involving 18,000 British viewers and broadcasters.

6 Feb 1989   Sky Television launch their DBS services on SES Astra-satellite.

Apr 1989	Launch of Discovery Channel. The Arts Channel closes.
27 Aug 1989	BSB launches its Marcopolo 1 satellite.
7 Nov 1989	Granada sells its longest running series *What The Papers Say* to the BBC, after 26 years on ITV and eight years on Channel Four.

Movers and Shakers

Alasdair Milne — BBC Director-General 1982-87

Michael Checkland — Milne's successor.

Marmaduke Hussey — Chairman of the Board of BBC Governors from 1986 – fired Milne.

Lord Thomson — IBA Chairman until 1988.

George Russell — Replaced Thomson.

John Whitney — Director-General of the IBA from 1982.

Anthony Simonds-Gooding — Chief Executive of BSB.

Michael Grade — Nephew of Lew. Controller BBC1 and Director of Programmes 1984-87, repopularised schedule before controversial leap to head Channel Four.

Bruce Gyngell — Australian Managing Director of TV-am who pitted himself against TV's trades unions.

Rupert Murdoch — Another Australian; later American.

Rewind: The Programmes of The 80s

Newsnight (BBC2, from 30 Jan 1980) — Extended late-night news programme which became compulsive viewing during the Falklands conflict, and spawned a host of high-profile presenters.

The Royal Wedding (BBC/ITV, 29 Jul 1981) — Prince Charles' wedding to Lady Diana Spencer was shown in 74 countries. And provided much footage for documentary use a decade later.

Brideshead Revisited (Granada, from 12 Oct 1981) — John Mortimer's adaptation of Evelyn Waugh's most popular novel starred Jeremy Irons, Anthony Andrews and Diana Quick. Derek Granger produced. The viewers loved it – but it was the last of the 'high culture' line for ITV.

Brideshead Revisited – languor 80s-style via the 30s

Game for a Laugh (LWT, 1981-85) — Started a run of 'people shows' that has not ended yet.

Tonight He's Yours (Showcable, 24 Dec 1981) — The first 'event' to be shown on British Pay-TV, this Rod Stewart concert with guest Tina Turner was recorded at the LA Forum a few days earlier.

...And It's Goodbye From Us (Southern, 31 Dec 1981) — Southern's final show. Fittingly, it overran.

The Boys From the Blackstuff (BBC2, from 10 Oct 1982) – Alan Bleasdale benchmark contemporary drama series about his tarmac-spreading gang who had originally appeared in the single play *The Black Stuff* two years earlier. Philip Saville directed at Pebble Mill.

Wogan (BBC1, from 15 Jan 1983) — Terry Wogan's long-running chat show started in the late night Saturday slot with Marcus Plantin as producer, before moving to its peaktime, three nights-a-week format, on 18 Feb 1985. Leading to a growth of chat shows in the 90s.

Blackadder (BBC1, from 15 Jun 1983) — Rowan Atkinson and Richard Curtis wrote this situation tragedy, which starred Atkinson with Brian Blessed, and Tony Robinson as Baldrick (with a 'cunning plan')

Auf Wiedersehen Pet (Central/Witzend, 1983-86) — The migrant builders showed the possibility of an independent making a mainstream popular programme.

Crimewatch UK (BBC1, 1984) — This tapped into an American trend for true crime programmes that was to prove popular in the UK. Nick Ross and Sue Cook presented.

Spitting Image (Central. from 1984) — Highly original puppets satirised national and international figures of the day.

'Allo 'Allo (BBC1, 1984-92) — The French resistance comedy by David Croft and Jeremy Lloyd proved that the sitcom was alive and well, if not very sophisticated.

East Enders, BBC's most popular soap, was a child of the 80s (plus *Marmaduke Hussey*)

East Enders (BBC1, from 19 Feb 1985) — The BBC's return to soap sparked an explosion of the genre.

Blind Date (LWT, from 1986) — One of LWT's most successful Saturday evening mass attractions. The Cilla Black-hosted voyeuristic gameshow throws a couple together and then allows viwers to observe the results.

Casualty (BBCl, from 6 Sep 1986) — BBC's medical series. A sustained ratings winner right into the 21st century.

The Singing Detective (BBC2, from 16 Nov 1986) — Michael Gambon starred in Dennis Potter's most personal, imaginative and award-winning mini-series.

ITN World News (ITN, from 30 Jan 1987 for Superchannel) — ITN's first non-ITV international bulletin, presented at first by John Suchet.

Inspector Morse (Central/Zenith, 1987-92) — *The* ratings-and-quality success of the 80s. What else had the power to make people stay home in the evenings?

VII
Must Try Harder
The 90s

Pressures
in a decade dedicated to change

Big Breakfast *– C4's wakeup*

The changes to and expansion of television in Britain that began as a trickle in the 70s and a full flow in the 80s turned into a raging flood in the last decade of the twentieth century. Of course the usual suspects were to be found - the BBC's new Royal Charter, a cause for much anxiety as the corporation entered the decade, was comfortably in place by the mid 90s; and mergers and acquisitions notwithstanding, the winners of the Great ITV Auction survived the mid-term financial review more or less unscathed.

But the decade started, in any case, with one of the most spectacular and prophetic coups in all of television's – not just British television's – colourful history. In March 1990 British Satellite Broadcasting (BSB) unveiled its five services, the first to be launched under the laboriously constructed international protocol for high-power direct-broadcast satellites (later, Direct To Home – DTH). A British first, government and IBA approved. Subscribers, equipped with the diamond-shaped 'squarial', would be able to receive channels devoted to sports, movies, pop music, general entertainment, topical and lifestyle matters, with high technical quality.

By November that same year, BSB was dead. A year earlier, Rupert Murdoch's Sky television had launched DTH at Britain, from a medium-power, Luxembourg-based satellite, Astra. Unblessed by any authority, mocked by numerous pundits for its likely reach and picture-quality and for the cheese-paring budgets behind its largely American programming, Sky was reckoned to be losing £2 million a week when the 'official' rival launched. It was now, declared BSB's Chief Executive, Anthony Simmonds-Gooding, looking down the barrel of "a well-funded gun". But by the autumn of 1990 the big-spending BSB, its marketing pitch muddied by the upstart, was 'bleeding red ink' at four times Sky's rate. Unknown to its executives, their shareholders (Granada, Anglia, Pearson and Virgin among them) defected.

Rupert Murdoch

On 2 November it was Murdoch's Sky News which broke the news of the merger. Though some BSB shareholders were to stay on board for the ride into the multi-channel future, its people, philosophy and economics were out of business. Rupert Murdoch now had well-heeled media players to share the financial risk in the renamed BSkyB, but he retained control, and Astra became the 'hot bird' to which other programme providers gravitated. Slowly but steadily the Astra package and the uptake of dishes grew until, in the autumn of 1993, BSkyB felt able to make the crucial leap to subscription funding, switching on a cash-flow that made terrestrial rivals gape, and created political waves over its buying power – of sports rights in particular.

Within two years substantial paybacks to shareholders had begun, and operating profits registered; in late 1995, BSkyB was opening more channels and welcoming its 5 millionth subscriber. With non-Sky Astra services also growing, they split a 34 per cent share of the audience in satellite/cable homes, and together took 9-plus per cent of the national cake. A new medium had been created, with Britain its test bed.

And in 1996 those Britons able to add £10 to subscriptions of up to £300 per annum eagerly participated in the first successful pay-per-view programme

Cable TV arrives in Britain

when Frank Bruno and Mike Tyson's prizefight was the first event to be offered on that basis by Sky.

By this time, multi-channel choice was the background against which all other players had to plan their own strategies, and there were more and more players as newspaper groups in particular sought stakes in the electronic future. But in 1990, horizons were necessarily narrower.

When the Thatcher government's market-force ideology – only somewhat moderated by the late influence of broadcasting minister David Mellor – was translated into the Broadcasting Act 1990, ITV faced a revolution as the new Independent Television Commission (a merger of the IBA and the Cable Authority) announced a new re-licensing round to be decided, all other things being equal, by the size of down payment and slice of future income that bidders were willing to donate to the government.

Before the end of 1990 Margaret Thatcher herself was gone, victim of a party coup caused by her own electoral unpopularity – but the die for the ITV auction was cast. On 16 October 1991, the ITC announced that from 1 January 1993, Thames Television would be replaced by Carlton, TVS by Meridian, TSW by Westcountry: the whole of southern England was to change hands. So

Yet another ITV detective series – *A Touch of Frost*

was the breakfast franchise, as TV-am lost out to what would become GMTV. The situation was rich with paradoxes and ironies. The biggest bid did not always win, as the ITC exercised the newly-narrowed 'quality threshold'. Some large companies – Central, Scottish – sensing they had no competitor, won with minimal bids, leaving them tens of millions better off than others in the new network. This was not the way the market-economists had foreseen it, though others had.

Even TV-am, the company that had led the ITV network in slashing costs and outfacing the unions, was not spared. Architect of this large-scale change, Prime Minister Margaret Thatcher, was appalled that the plan (conceived mainly to punish Thames for its failure to toe her political line) had backfired in the case of her favoured breakfast channel, and wrote a famously publicised personal letter of apology to TV-am's Managing Director, Bruce Gyngell.

But even all that was, in a sense, just the surface eruption of an industry undergoing seismic change. The new economics dictated new structures. Once-integrated companies now split their broadcasting, programme production and sales functions. Some new ITV licensees were to be publisher-broadcasters, not producers. The new system would soon permit takeovers and mergers of and between ITV companies. Some suggested it must in the end come down to a single 'ITV UK plc'. Already the scheduling and commissioning function was to pass to a new body, the ITV Network Centre.

The BBC was relatively unscathed by the new Act, but not by the political climate. With the governors' sacking of Alasdair Milne in 1987, and his replacement by Michael Checkland, a career manager, the corporation too was being focussed on the bottom line. But Checkland did not act fast enough for the chairman, Marmaduke Hussey. As his five-year term was heading for renewal the board delivered a vote of no-confidence, offering a one-year extension before his deputy, John Birt, would take over. This lame-duck period reached an unprecedented climax in October 1992, when Checkland, at an RTS symposium, publicly mocked Hussey as being too old. The government gave the chairman another term.

Birt, who as deputy had vigorously overseen a merger of news and current affairs, with some well-known journalists displaced by outside blood – now brought the same single-mindedness to the task of creating internal market disciplines within the BBC, implementing the Producer Choice process he had already inaugurated, whereby every part of the broadcasting process was costed and much opened up to outside competition. Making this system work proved as difficult as winning the staff to support it along with the new regime.

One seminal outcome of all these pressures for change, across both BBC and ITV, was that, while management consultants had five years rich in gravy, workers at all levels faced deep insecurity. The commercial companies' rush to rationalisation slashed staff jobs; the BBC, en route to that, took refuge in short-term contracts.

Simultaneously, a galaxy of ITV executives became paper millionaires – soon to be converted to cash, as the takeovers started; the Chief Executive of C4, Michael Grade, was given a greatly enhanced 'golden handcuffs' contract; even the BBC's new Director-General was revealed to be on a freelance contract, paid through his private company with concomitant tax benefits.

Such moves, to the worldly-wise, merely reflected the value of the available talent as a new raft of movers and shakers came into the game. The incumbents of the 80s learned to make new friends. Carlton's victory put Michael Green (the enigmatic businessman who, years earlier, had bid for Thames under the old rules and been rebuffed) in a prime position. Clive Hollick, the 'socialist peer' who paid bonuses in bullion, headed MAI, Meridian's parent. Granada, the ultimate cradle-to-grave company, saw David Plowright yield to Gerry Robinson and Charles Allen – 'caterers' according to their business CVs, but soon to make their marks.

Others redeployed. At BSkyB Murdoch paired his tough, retiring Australian boss, Sam Chisholm with David Elstein (ex-Thames Programme Chief) who would provide the new medium with an agile, articulate advocate. Marcus Plantin emerged from LWT to head the ITV Network Centre, while Greg Dyke would cash in his options and head for the independent sector, as Pearson grew its business.

Granada bought LWT (for £775m); the publisher-contractor, Carlton, won Central (for £758m); new slim Meridian was paired with Anglia. But while market forces worked very well for some, as the decade progressed there were worries about who was training the next generations and what future instability was risked by organisations reliant on workers contracted job by job – even whether in-house production might have its benefits, after all.

In all of this, programmes carried on being made and transmitted. For ITV in 1993 the new Network Centre came in fighting, its ratings riding high on well-established drama hits, just as the BBC seemed to have lost the popular touch, with its new economics being much blamed. But a couple of years later the cycle had swung once more, with ITV seeking renewal and multiplying soap-operas as its audiences seemed most vulnerable to satellite nibbling. The BBC's new titles, backed by the substantial cash the economies were indeed delivering, brought renewed acclaim just as the softer-line Major government was delivering a new Royal Charter.

Even the smaller channels were thriving, with a canny (C4 said 'copycat') BBC2 finding a healthy audience share, and C4 selling its own airtime to unexpected effect, increasing its share of the commercial audience even as it campaigned noisily against the funding formula that saw an ever-growing amount being handed over to ITV.

In their efforts to reconsolidate their positions in an era of promised multiplicity, the terrestrial quartet were all helped by the tardiness of that choice in coming. The Astra proposition apart, the technological future came more slowly than some of those consultants had predicted.

For those with visions of a cabled society, the leap to DTH satellite came as a mixed blessing: it offered cable operators a more attractive range of programming to relay, but gave the consumer an alternative, instantly available, medium. After a stagnant decade British cable was eyed by North American operators, and the regulatory path cleared for their dollars to pour in. New

The Wedding of the Year: Darcy and Elizabeth finally tie the knot in the BBC's *Pride and Prejudice*, returning old-fashioned romance to the nervy nineties

names – TCI, CableWest – joined the industry lexicon. But telephony, not television, proved the attractive option and, though the speed of building picked up, average penetration of homes passed stuck at not much above 20 per cent.

The drive to digitalisation was to be a hallmark of the 90s, with radical implications for everything from news-gathering to promo videos, transmission techniques to editing suites, with British software wizardry frequently at the cutting-edge. The manipulation of images matching speed with sophistication had instant impact for the viewer.

Other potential users proved more elusive, for a variety of reasons. The great white hope as the decade dawned was high-definition television (HDTV), already more than a decade in the labs of Europe and Japan. But as the reality got near enough for a compatible standard to become a transnational political issue, the domestic hardware industry, increasingly hungry for a new product, went cool on cost and size. Widescreen formats could sell a new generation of receivers, the new wisdom reckoned, but HDTV's definition, so awesome to the professionals, was a trimming too far for the couch-potato.

On a different technological level, digital compression offered more effective use of the terrestrial spectrum – more channels for new services. 'Multiplexing' joined the broadcasting industry's daily jargon. In the wake of the BSkyB debacle, the government – whose philosophy had now evolved to the position of making regulated space available (at a price) for entrepreneurs to utilise as they judged the market demanded – found room, first for a fifth terrestrial analogue channel, then for a clutch of terrestrial digital ones, to be fed to the consumer in a complex, interwoven stream.

As for digital terrestrial (DTT), 1996 dawned with the industry at large still uncertain as to how the government's masterplan would work – what combination of existing services, new services, subscription, widescreen, might be possible? – and even less sure whether there would prove to be a business in it. Mr Murdoch had already booked his digital space – on the digital Astra bird.

That was the theory. In April 1992 however, the ITC invited bids for Channel 5, got just one, and rejected its business plan. Urged on by Parliament, it tried again in November 1994, and a year later awarded the licence to a group formed by MAI and Pearson, having rejected the highest bidder.

Door-to-door retuning of many thousands of VCRs - the bit that rather took the technological gloss off the enterprise - proved successful despite a handful of scare stories in an unsympathetic press, and the new service was launched by the Spice Girls on 31st March 1997.

The enforced technical constraints resulting from the 'shoehorning' of an extra channel into a frequency plan designed to accommodate only four caused a  number of complaints of poor or non-existent reception from viewers in some key heavily populated areas. But within weeks of its launch Channel 5 secured a place on Astra, and the addition of satellite and cable viewers alleviated some of the initial problems, as did a number of later refinements to the power and quantity of its transmitters. These coupled with a refinement of the schedules improved the initially disappointing ratings.

The ITV companies were now effectively whittled down to just seven with Carlton's acquisition of Westcountry for £85m; STV's purchase of Grampian for £105m, (not to mention its 15 per cent of Ulster) Granada's £711m takeover of Yorkshire-TyneTees and a near-20 per cent stake in HTV costing United News and Media (formerly MAI) £73.7m.

Consolidation wasn't the exclusive province of ITV, for the cable companies also entered into a series of mergers until there were just three - Cable & Wireless, NTL and Telewest. As for digital – Rupert Murdoch predictably stole a march on the planned terrestrial services by launching his 200+ digital channel service on satellite. For the first time this included most of the existing 'free' terrestrial services, now able to transmit in widescreen.

The BBC added to its pair of channels a whole new raft of licence-supported services, including a 24-hour news channel, BBC Parliament, BBC Knowledge and BBC Choice. The latter effectively a BBC-3 – was provided in four different versions, for the first time allowing satellite viewers outside the nations to regularly view programmes designed for viewers in Scotland, Northern Ireland and Wales wherever they happened to be in the Kingdom. And in a partnership with US cable giant Flextech, the BBC also launched a number of new subscription services under the 'UK' brand.

Channel 4 unveiled its movie service – FilmFour – and was joined by Channel 5 on Sky Digital, but the huge Carlton/Granada stake in ON Digital's terrestrial service meant that ITV as a family refused to climb on to Sky's rival platform.

When Ulrika Jonsson finally turned ON on, the mix of channels it offered included some from major shareholder Carlton, as well as the existing ITV services and two new ones - ITV2 for viewers in England and Wales, and S2 for viewers in Scotland, with a promised second channel for Ulster early in the new millennium, and GMTV2 incorporated in all of these. Initial problems with the supply of decoder boxes provided ON with some anxious moments during its early months, but figures proved better than expected with 110,000 subscribers in the first four months.

It is of course too soon for history to judge the success of these digital services – initial take-up of both was modest and although widescreen was seen as an incentive, the high cost and limited availability of suitable new receivers held down progress.

Heralded as "the country's fifth and last 'free' television service" Channel 5 was not in fact to be the last to launch on old-fashioned analogue UHF. As the big boys fought pitched battles in the digital domain, a handful of tiny local television operators took advantage of new regulations that allowed

FilmFour launches (1 Nov 1998)
with *Gabriel Byrne* in *The Usual Suspects*

for limited additional services where spare frequencies could be found.

First to hold a four-year "Restricted Service Licence" was TV 12 on the Isle of Wight, providing an alternative of truly local programmes to those islanders prepared to invest in new aerials. TV 12 was joined by similar small-scale operations in Oxford and Lanarkshire before the end of the decade, with more such channels planned in the coming years.

And while all this was happening, the men (and very occasionally women) at the top played their never-ending games of musical chairs. To chronicle all such movements in the decade would require a rather tedious volume of its own, but there were two major surprises towards the end of the 90s. One was the decision of the charismatic Michael Grade to quit not only Channel 4 but the television business in January 1997. He became executive chairman of bingo and entertainment group First Leisure Corporation, and was succeeded at Channel 4 by former BBC2 controller Michael Jackson.

Second was the appointment of former boss of LWT and latterly Pearson Television, the equally charismatic Greg Dyke as the new Director-General of the BBC, a position he formally took up early in the year 2000. His style of management is rather different to that of his predecessor. "Running companies is about leadership and not about management. Don't be aloof, be available. Don't consider yourself better or different. East in the canteen, talk to the guys. It could be them, not you: you're lucky." - that's what he said in 1994.

As the BBC mounted one of its most ambitious live programmes in television history, the 26 hour extravaganza, *2000 Today*, which saw the new year begin around the globe through the eyes of an extraordinary plethora of outside broadcasts, webcasting, the main challenger for the eyes and minds of Britain's viewers was still just around the corner.

Selected Dates

2 Nov 1990	BSB merges with Sky to become British Sky Broadcasting.
1 Mar 1991	TV listings monopoly ends. New magazines mushroom – *Radio Times* wins.
3 Feb 1992	Outcry as David Plowright is forced to resign as Executive Chairman of Granada after 'fundamental disagreement' with the board.

2 Jun 1992	BSkyB and BBC announce deal with the FA to show Premiere League football live on Sky Sports, with recorded highlights on BBC1.
27 Feb 1993	Alan Yentob named Controller, BBC1.
2 Apr 1993	Michael Jackson named Controller, BBC2.
31 Dec 1993	Satellite/cable company Flextech acquires UA Programming from TCI, who take a majority stake in Flextech.
25 Jan 1995	BBC launches international satellite channels, BBC World and BBC Prime.
16 Feb 1995	Mirror Television, owners of Live TV, buy the competing cable-only channel Wire TV. And close it.
1 Oct 1995	Disney Channel launches on Astra.
28 Oct 1995	ITC awards Channel 5 licence to Channel 5 Broadcasting – though they weren't the highest bidder.
31 Mar 1997	Channel 5 launches.
1 Apr 1997	The Broadcasting Standards Council merges with the Broadcasting Complaints Commission to form the Broadcasting Standards Commission.
2 May 1997	Michael Jackson succeeds Michael Grade as chief executive of Channel 4.
24 May 1997	Alan Yentob is made the BBC's Director of Television, in charge of BBC1, BBC2 and the new digital services.
6 Sep 1997	The funeral of Diana Princess of Wales is the biggest outside broadcast in television history.
9 Nov 1997	BBC News 24 launched on cable.
23 Sep 1998	BBC Choice begins on Sky Digital. 1 Oct 1998 Sky Digital launches to 20,000 subscribers.
31 Oct 1998	First of the 'RSL' local TV stations, TV 12 goes on the air on the Isle of Wight.
1 Nov 1998	FilmFour launches on satellite and cable. 15 Nov 1998 ON Digital starts transmitting its services. 7 Dec 1998 Start of ITV2 via ON Digital in England & Wales.
May 1999	S2 available in Scotland via ON Digital.
1 Jun 1999	Launch of digital channel BBC Knowledge.
5 Mar 1999	The final edition of News at Ten is transmitted.

Some People of The 90s

John Birt — BBC Director-General throughout the decade.

Sir Robin Biggum — Chairman of the ITC, took over from Sir George Russell.

Michael Jackson — Began the decade as Controller of BBC2 and ended it as Chief Executive. Channel 4.

David Elstein — Programme maker turned executive, moved from Sky to be Chief Executive of Channel 5.

Dawn Airey — First Director of Programmes at Channel 5.

Alan Yentob — From Controller, BBC1 to the BBC's Director of Television.

Adam Singer — Chairman and Chief Executive of US giant Flextech, and son of Aubrey, former Controller, BBC2.

Richard Eyre — Former boss of Capital Radio, joined ITV as chief executive in July 1997.

David Liddiment — ITV Network Director of Programmes.

Peter Salmon — Controller, BBC1 from 1997.

Jane Root — Controller, BBC2 taking over from Michael Jackson.

Mark Booth — Successor to Sam Chisholm as head of BSkyB.

Andrea Wonfor — Managing Director, Granada Productions – described in the terms of an RTS award as "one of the most respected and liked executives in British television. A Gazza in tights."

Programming The 90s

Prime Suspect (Granada, from 1991) — Helen Mirren as Detective Inspector Jane Tennison gripped the nation.

Noel's House Party (BBC1, from 1991) — Noel Edmonds' highly popular entertainment format introduced Mr. Blobby to the unsuspecting public.

GBH (GBH Films/Channel 4, 1991) — Alan Bleasdale's 10-hour long, political, funny and dark drama series was a major critical success.

The Darling Buds of May (Excelsior Group Productions / Yorkshire TV, 1991) — H. E. Bates' stories of simple family pleasures set in the Kent countryside of the 50s starred David Jason, Pam Ferris and Catherine Zeta Jones.

Absolutely Fabulous (BBC2, 1992) — Tales of drugs, alcohol and self-indulgence in Jennifer Saunders' lauded sitcom that transferred to BBC1 in 1995 and re-established Joanna Lumley as a character actress.

Mr Bean (Tiger Aspect for ITV) — Rowan Atkinson's absurd creation made few selective appearances, adding to his appeal.

The Big Breakfast (Planet 24/ Channel 4, from 28 Sep 1992) — The original team of Gaby Roslin, Chris Evans and Paula Yates replaced ITN's Channel Four Daily with an instant innovative hit.

Wallace and Gromit

Wallace and Gromit (Aardman Animations for BBC from 1992) — A handful of brilliant animations (starting with A Grand Day Out) won audiences, acclaim and an Oscar.

Cracker (Granada, from 1993) — Robbie Coltraine and writer Jimmy McGovern garnered awards from this psychological thriller series.

The National Lottery (BBC1, from 19 Nov 1994) — In an astonishing variety of shapes and forms, this twice-weekly event usually proves a worthwhile ratings device for the BBC.

Four Weddings and a Funeral (Channel 4, 1995) — C4 made a huge return on its original investment of £400,000 in this Film on Four, the biggest box-office success of any British film.

Pride and Prejudice (BBC1, from 24 Sep 1995) — Andrew Davies' adaptation of the Jane Austen novel confirmed TV's rediscovery of costume-drama

Father Ted (Channel 4, from 1995) — Three series of award winning sitcom built around three absurd Irish priests and their housekeeper ended with the tragic death at the age of 45 of its star, Dermot Morgan.

TFI Friday (Ginger Productions for Channel 4, from 9 Feb 1996) — Official title "Thank Four it's Friday", Chris Evans' weekly live party.

Ballykissangel (BBC1, from 11 Feb 1996) — All began when an English priest (played by Stephen Tomkinson) was despatched to rural Ireland; after which Sunday nights were never the same.

*Radio Times: Look **Who**'s back on Saturday night*
13-19 November 1999

ITV papers spanning four decades

The Teletubbies (Ragdoll Productions for BBC, from 31 Mar 1997) — Anne Wood's creation for under-fives – Tinky Winky, Dipsy, Laa Laa and Po grabbed the imagination of children of all ages the world over.

Jonathan Creek (BBC1, from 10 May 1997) — David Renwick's original detective series starring comedian Alan Davies in the title role alongside Caroline Quentin as cohort Madelaine Magellan.

Who Wants to be A Millionaire? (Celador Productions for ITV, from 1998) — High-stakes gameshow shown on consecutive nights and hosted by Chris Tarrant.

2000 Today (BBC1, 31 Dec 1999) — The 28-hour long final show of the 90s was a tour de force for presenter Gaby Roslin and Executive Editor Avril McRory.

TV in Print

This small volume has culled a considerable amount of information from a very wide variety of sources. In particular, the once annual *BBC Year Books* (1928 – 1987) and equivalent *ITV Handbooks* (1963 – 1988) have been heavily plundered, as have the volumes of *Radio Times* and *TV Times*, as well as the now defunct regional ITV programme magazines, *TV Guide, Television Weekly, The Viewer, TV Post, Look Westward, TV World, Channel Viewer*, and *Wales TV*. More recent history has been culled from issues of *Television (The Journal of the Royal Television Society)* within whose pages most of this book made its first appearance.

FOR FURTHER READING

Of the published histories, the most comprehensive are:–

The History of Broadcasting in the United Kingdom (Vols. l-5) — *Prof. Asa Briggs* (OUP, 1961–1995); **The BBC – the First Fifty Years** — *Prof. Asa Briggs* (OUP, 1985) – although Briggs' books actually only deal with the history of the BBC and skim effortlessly over ITV and commercial radio.

The BBC – 70 years of broadcasting — *John Cain* (BBC 1992) is lighter, less academic in its approach, and much better illustrated.

Independent Television in Britain (Vols 1–2) — *Bernard Sendall* (Macmillan Press, 1982–1983); goes into plodding detail on the construction of the ITV system. **(Vols. 3–4)** by *Jeremy Potter* (Macmillan Press, 1989–1990) cover the period 1968–1980.

The early days of 30-line TV are adequately chronicled in three books:–

Sermons Soap and Television — *John Logie Baird's* memoirs (Royal Television Society, 1988).

Television Baird — *Margaret Baird* (Haum, Cape Town, 1973).

Vision Warrior — *Tom McArthur* and *Peter Waddell* (The Orkney Press, 1990) – a revised version of the work originally published by Hutchinson under the title, **The Secret Life of John Logie Baird.**

The development of the new medium is amusingly described in:–

Here's Looking at You — *Bruce Norman* (BBC/RTS, 1984) which paints a picture of pre-war conditions.

Coming To You – Live! — *Denis Norden, Sybil Harper* and *Norma Gilbert* (Methuen, 1985) which dispenses many postwar anecdotes.

Behind the Screen — ed. *Carel Enkelaar* (NOS/Strengholt, Holland, 1979) tells the story of Eurovision's first 25 years.

Memories of Tyne Tees Television — *Geoff Phillips* (GP Electronic Services, 1998) recounts the early days of Newcastle's ITV station.

Less amusing (but none the less interesting) are:–

Television's Story and Challenge — *Derek Horton* (Harrap, 1951).

Thirty Years in Cable TV – Reminiscences of a Pioneer — *Kenneth J. Easton* (Pioneer Publications, Toronto, 1980) which absorbingly covers in detail the birth of cable in London as well as North America.

TV File — ed. *David McKie* (Panther Record, 1967) is a good account of the 1967 ITA refranchising process.

Television's Greatest Hits — *Paul Gambaccini and Rod Taylor* (BBC Network Books, 1993) an excellent and reliable source of programme information covering three decades.

More contemporary accounts of the state of the medium may be found in:–

The Third Age of Broadcasting — ed. *Brian Wenham* (Faber & Faber, 1982).

One Day in the Life of Television — Ed. *Sean Day-Lewis* (Grafton Books, 1989).

And an exceptionally readable and highly personal account of the whole era is:–

It Seemed Like A Good Idea At The Time — *Michael Grade* (Macmillan, 1999).

Glossary of Abbreviations

AEF	Allied Expeditionary Forces
ARTV	Associated Rediffusion Television
a.s.m	assistant stage manager
ATV	Associated TeleVision
BARB	Broadcasters Audience Research Board
BBC	British Broadcasting Corporation
BCC	Broadcasting Complaints Commission
BSB	British Satellite Broadcasting
BSkyB	British Sky Broadcasting
CBC	Canadian Broadcasting Corporation
CBS	Columbia Broadcasting System
CEO	Chief Executive Officer
CPS	Cathode Potential Stabiliser
CSO	Colour Separation Overlay
DBS	Direct Broadcasting Satellite
DTH	Direct-to-Home
DTT	Digital Terrestrial Television
EBU	European Broadcasting Union
ENG	Electronic News Gathering
EMI	Electrical and Musical Industries
GMTV	Good Morning Television
HDTV	high-definition television
HTV	Harlech Television
IBA	Independent Broadcasting Authority
ITA	Independent Television Authority
ITN	Independent Television News
ITV	Independent Television
LE	Light Entertainment
LWT	London Weekend Television
MD	Managing Director

MTV	Music Television
NBC	National Broadcasting Company
NTC	National Television Council
NTSC	National Television Systems Committee
OB	Outside Broadcast
PAL	Phase Alternation Line
RAI	Radiotelevisione Italiana (Italian Broadcasting Corporation)
REP	Renters, Exhibitors and Producers
RSL	Restricted Service Licence
RTE	Radio Telefís Éireann
RTS	Royal Television Society
S4C	Sianel Pedwar Cymru (Welsh Fourth Channel)
SES	Société Européenne des Satellites
STV	Scottish Television
TCI	Tele Communications Incorporated
TEN	The Entertainment Network
TTT	Tyne Tees Television
TWW	Television Wales & West
UA	United Artists
UHF	Ultra-High-Frequency
VCR	Video Cassette Recording
VHF	Very High Frequency
VHS	Video Home System
Y-TTTV	Yorkshire-Tyne Tees Television
YTV	Yorkshire Television